A LONG HALF HOUR

For Trevor

Wishing you all the best for
Christmas 2010 and for the New Year.

Phil.

A LONG HALF HOUR

Six Cricketers Remembered

Stephen Chalke

FAIRFIELD BOOKS

Fairfield Books
17 George's Road, Bath BA1 6EY
Tel 01225-335813

The photograph on the back of the book
is of Sheepscombe Cricket Ground in Gloucestershire.
Ken Biddulph is the fielder nearest to the camera.

Photographs appear by kind permission, as follows: Arthur Milton,
from David Foot; Geoff Edrich, from PA Photos; Bomber Wells,
from Mary Wells; Dickie Dodds and Sonny Avery, from Getty Images;
Eric Hill and Harold Gimblett, from the Somerset Cricket Museum.

First published 2010

ISBN 978 0 9560702 6 5

Printed and bound in Great Britain by
Midway Colour Print, Trowbridge, Wiltshire

Contents

About the author

Stephen Chalke took up writing about cricket in 1997. His first book, *Runs in the Memory*, a portrait of county cricket in the 1950s, was Frank Keating's Sports Book of the Year in *The Guardian*, and he has followed this with several further books about cricket's past.

For the past nine years he has been a regular contributor to *The Wisden Cricketer* magazine, and he has also written for *The Times* and *The Independent*. A collection of his articles, *The Way It Was*, won the National Sporting Club's Cricket Book of the Year award.

Born in 1948, he still plays cricket regularly and has written a fictionalised account of his experiences: *Now I'm 62 – The Diary of an Ageing Cricketer*.

He runs his own publishing company, **Fairfield Books**, specialising mainly in cricket. Further details of its titles can be found on page 128.

Introduction

Here are six men who played county cricket in England. They span the years from May 1946, when Geoff Edrich first played for Lancashire, to July 1974, when Arthur Milton last played for Gloucestershire.

I have written several books about this period of English cricket, based mostly on conversations with the players themselves. They were the years in which I grew up, and they now seem long ago and far away, a distant age in which so much was not as it is now. I don't want to say that it was a better age, or a worse age, just that it was different – and that we should not forget our past. We are always the children of what went before.

I must have sat and talked with more than a hundred cricketers who played in those years, and I have enjoyed every conversation. Several times I have written a full-length book with one person; more often I have written brief articles. The six men in this volume, other than that they all played cricket in England in those years and that they have all now died, have one simple thing in common. I have met and written about them all, and I have been left with a feeling that what I have written has not done full justice to what they have told me.

Because I have written about them before, there will be passages in each chapter which have appeared previously in my published work, but there is much that is new. I have also approached the writing a little differently, telling something of my contacts with each of them. In this respect there is a sub-theme about oral history that runs through the book.

My reasons for choosing these six are various. Some have fascinated me with the individuality of their character, some have challenged me with the distinctiveness of their beliefs, some have entertained me with their great fund of stories. They have all caught my imagination.

There are few well-known names here. Only one of the subjects, Arthur Milton, played Test cricket. Yet, as I have found so often in the fourteen years I have been listening to cricketers, it is not always the most famous people who have the most interesting things to say.

I start with Ken Biddulph because that is where I started.

Stephen Chalke

Bath, October 2010

Cricket

with

**Former
Somerset
Professional**

Ken Biddulph

1

KEN BIDDULPH

A long half hour

Kenneth David Biddulph

Born: Chingford, 29 May 1932

Died: Oxford, 7 January 2003

"Half an hour? You can't do anything in half an hour."

It was the autumn of 1993. I was 45 years old, and my summer's cricket had not gone well. For the first time I had developed back problems, and in 22 games I had taken just 23 wickets. I was wondering if it was time to call it a day.

I worked in adult education. "You're never too old to learn," I told the students. So, shaking off my end-of-season depression, I decided to take my own advice: get some winter coaching, see if I could learn some new skills.

That summer we had moved to Bath, and I was not sure how to find a suitable coach. Somehow, after several phone calls, I found myself ringing a Ken Biddulph, who lived somewhere in the Cotswolds. Apparently he had played for Somerset.

I looked in *Wisden* – 'Births and Deaths of Cricketers' – and there he was: *Biddulph, K.D. (Som.) b May 29, 1932*

"I understand what you want," he told me. "If I can get you a few more runs, a few more wickets, keep you enjoying the game for a few more years, you'll be happy, won't you?"

"Yes, exactly."

So far, so reassuring.

"What did you have in mind?"

"I can get away early on Fridays. Maybe I could come up for half an hour with you each week."

"Half an hour?" he repeated with disbelief. "You can't do anything in half an hour."

"Well, an hour perhaps."

He rang back three days later.

"Stephen? I've booked the Stratford Park Leisure Centre in Stroud for Friday afternoon, 4 to 5.30."

My apprehension was growing. At the end of a long week's work, including two late evenings, I would have to rush home from Bristol, collect my kit and change, drive the 30 miles to Stroud, then bowl for an hour and a half on my own in a net. The prospect daunted me, and I started to wonder whether he realised just how ordinary a cricketer I was.

It was ten to four when I made my way, cricket bag in hand, to the main entrance of the leisure centre. There I was greeted by a tall, slim and very erect man. He had a good head of wavy, silver-grey hair and wore a Somerset blazer over some old-fashioned cricket whites.

"Stephen? Nice to meet you. I've got some good news. There's nobody in after us till six o'clock."

He asked me to show him my bowling action. So I ran in and bowled a few balls. "It's very good," he said. Then he proceeded to make some alterations. He got me picking my knees up higher. He made some footmarks with chalk on the floor and asked me to land in them. He had me delivering the ball more side-on, with a greater swivel of the hips and my front arm reaching higher. In no time I was so disorientated by the changes that the ball started to fly all over the place: into the side of the net, even onto its roof.

"That's much more like it, Stephen. Now we're getting somewhere."

I had my doubts, but there was an air of authority mixed in with the genial enthusiasm and I decided to trust him.

By six o'clock I was exhausted. The staff at the centre pushed back the net, and the room was turned over to five-a-side football. Ken collected up his equipment, and I followed him up to the balcony where, with my shirt dripping wet on my back, we stood, half-watching the footballers.

It was the fifth of November, and I had promised to go with the family to a fireworks display at Bath University. I soon realised, however, that for Ken we had only completed the warm-up session. The main fun of the occasion, for him, was to regale me with stories of his days as a Somerset cricketer.

As a boy I had watched Hampshire, where my first hero was the bespectacled Roy Marshall, a white West Indian who thought nothing of hitting the first ball of the match for four. He would cut in-swingers to the third man boundary or drive the ball imperiously through the covers. It all seemed so easy, and there was never much running between the wickets, just a blaze of boundaries. What a groan went round the ground when he was out!

"Roy was a great bat," Ken said. "He used to hit me all over the place. I remember getting him out at Bournemouth. For 212. Second new ball. What a wonderful player. I used to lie awake the night before the Hampshire match, dreading having to bowl at him."

I was enchanted. I was no longer a boy sitting among the spectators, watching distant figures; Ken was transporting me across the boundary into the world of the players themselves.

"I got him out for nought once," he went on. "In the first over. I think I had him caught at short leg."

When I got home, I looked for it in the old *Wisdens* I had kept from my childhood.

Taunton. 22 July 1959
R.E. Marshall c Lomax b Biddulph 0
Biddulph 27.3 overs, 5 wickets for 49 runs

"I'm like a cat with ten tails; I've got Roy out first over for nothing. At the end of the over I go down to field at fine leg, my usual place, for Bill Alley to come up and bowl. And there was an entrance down at that side, and the old turnstile was clicking. People coming in. There was a group came in, and one of them turned and looked up at the scoreboard. 'I say,' he says, 'Marshall's out. I've come all the way from Southampton to see Marshall bat, and some silly bugger's got him out.' Never mind. It didn't spoil my day. I'd got Roy out for nought, and that was one of my great ambitions in life.

"Many years later I went down to Taunton to play for the Somerset Over-50s, and who should I see in our dressing room, the home team, but Roy Marshall? I'd forgotten he was living down there. He had a pub up the road and was chairman of the cricket committee. I could have kissed him. 'Do you know, Roy? I've dreamed about this moment. Being on your side.' 'But you used to get me out.' 'Eventually,' I said."

Talk of Hampshire led him on to their Old Etonian captain, Colin Ingleby-Mackenzie, how the Hampshire twelfth man was forever running messages to the local bookmaker and coming onto the outfield with the latest race results. Early one summer, Ken told me, Ingleby-Mackenzie hit a very quick hundred. In those days there was a prize of £100 for the fastest century of the summer, and he managed to get a bookmaker to give him odds of 4/1 that his own effort would be beaten before the summer was out. He placed a bet of £25, ensuring that one way or another he would finish up with £100. Later in the summer – against Somerset, inevitably – he beat it himself, so finishing up with two cheques for £100.

Bournemouth. 18 June 1958

A.C.D. Ingleby-Mackenzie not out 113 in 61 minutes

Biddulph 2 wickets for 82 runs

"In the evening we were eating in the hotel," Ken said. "The Hampshire team were on the next table, and the waiter came over. 'Excuse me, gentlemen,' he said. 'Everything is on Mr Ingleby-Mackenzie.'"

The stories continued to flow. Fred Trueman, Colin Cowdrey, Frank Tyson, the cricketers of my childhood were coming alive, one after another. Not just the cricketers, either, but their whole way of life.

"We had one year when we went everywhere by train. Can you imagine going by train from Taunton? We spent about 400 hours at Bristol Temple Meads, waiting for connections. You'd finish a game at 4.30 or 5 on the final day, then you had to go to Bristol before you could get anywhere. By the time you got to the hotel, you wouldn't get a hot meal; you'd be lucky if you got a sandwich. I remember arriving at Old Trafford after three in the morning.

"Most years we used to go round in cars. Bill Alley used to drive a Morris 1000 van. Painted yellow and black. It was known as the Wasp. And he used to carry the bags. At the end of the game we'd all leave our bags beside Bill's van. He insisted that he would load them up, to get the right balance, so off we'd go and leave him there. We'd drive as fast as we could and, when we got to the hotel, there would be Bill waiting for us. 'Where have you been then, lads? There's a good dinner.'

"He was caught speeding once in Nottingham. 'It's like this, officer,' he said. 'We were in the field all day yesterday. I bowled 38 overs, I'm tired and we were late getting to the hotel. And we're bound to lose the toss today.' He nearly had the policeman in tears. He finished up getting to the ground with a police escort. That could only happen to Bill."

My damp shirt dried out, and I hardly noticed that my back was stiffening up. The five-a-side football ended, and the badminton nets came out. When I finally looked at my watch, it was nearly half past seven. I found a phone box and rang home. "I don't think I'm going to make it for the fireworks. You'll have to go on without me."

I paid Ken £20. By the time he had settled up for the net, and adding in our time on the balcony, I think he must have earned about £1.50 an hour. But that was Ken for you.

"See you next Friday, Stephen."

Friday afternoon became the highlight of my week.

In the second session Ken had a long look at my batting, getting me to wait longer for the ball, play with a bent front knee, rock my arms as if a baby were cradled in them. To emphasise all this, he would break into a Frank Sinatra impersonation: *'Cause nice 'n' easy does it every time.*

"My highest score for Somerset was 41," he told me on the balcony afterwards. "At Southend. Colin Atkinson and I put on 75 for the last wicket. It was the last day. I think we needed 70 or so to make them bat again. And we just got them. We weren't very popular. We had a long journey, all the team had changed out of their whites, and Bill had loaded up the Wasp, ready to get off. And we had to go out to field for about one over. I remember Colin McCool pulling his whites over his everyday clothes. Old Bill went mad. 'What on earth were you two doing? We could be halfway to Taunton by now.'"

Southend. 19 August 1960
K.D. Biddulph b Hurd 41
Essex, 4 for no wicket, won by 10 wickets

Some years later the *Cricketer* magazine published an extraordinary table that recorded 'Runs of Not Out Innings in English First-Class Cricket', and Ken's name – much to his amusement – was near the top. It turned out that the Southend dismissal brought to an end a sequence of nine innings, spread across twelve matches and seven weeks, in which he had not been out. "Well, fancy that," he said. "I never thought I'd get into *The Cricketer* for my batting."

The weeks passed. Slowly the accuracy of my bowling returned and with it some fresh nip off the wicket. One week Ken set up a video camera so that I could see my bowling action for myself. Unfortunately the only television screens in the centre were in the gym upstairs, and there was a resentful atmosphere in the room when the runners and cyclists, pounding away to a video of *Boom Shake The Room*, suddenly found themselves staring at repeated sequences of me running in to bowl.

"You're looking a bit like Derek Shackleton," Ken said, summoning up another of my childhood Hampshire heroes. Thereafter, much to my delight, he would occasionally refer to me as 'Shack'.

In the following weeks Ken started to introduce other players. First there was Alistair, a 15-year-old with some promise. The first time I bowled to him, I let slip a long hop that he crashed with such force that, even with the net in the way, he set off the centre's fire alarm. We had to evacuate the building till the fire service arrived and gave the all-clear.

Then there was Ed, a young fast bowler who could get the ball to bounce up nastily at my rib cage; Paul, an older left-armer who seemed to direct every delivery at my big toe and talked endlessly about all the bad umpiring decisions he had suffered the previous summer; and Mark, a surveyor who almost fell over backwards as he bowled but had the ball swinging both ways, early and late. It was a challenge to bowl to their standard, and a greater challenge to survive with the bat.

The Stratford Park Leisure Centre had its problems. There was a high staff turnover, and the facilities cried out for some tender loving care. The nets never ran easily on their rails, and the mats had seen better days. But it did not matter; we had Ken Biddulph, in his immaculate whites, and he brought his own atmosphere with him.

"Now then, young man," he would say to me, and immediately my ageing limbs were raring to go. "There's a new batsman down there. Make him play." I would select a shining ball from his box and send down four away-swingers outside the off-stump. "If I'd wasted the new ball like that," he would tell me cheerfully, "I'd have had Maurice Tremlett's boot up my backside. Come on now. Bowl at the stumps."

He loved our enthusiasm, though he did occasionally get irritated with Alistair who had a certain adolescent lethargy. "What's the matter with these youngsters? I reckon it's taken him eight minutes to get his pads on. When I was his age, I'd have been that keen, I'd have had them on in thirty seconds." He turned to me. "Right now, young man, get those arms up high."

For the others the net was four till six, but for me it was always four till seven-thirty, sometimes even eight.

"When I was sixteen," Ken told me one day, "I started going to Alf Gover's for coaching. The *Evening News* sponsored free places for promising young players. There must have been a dozen of us who went on to play county cricket. Malcolm Heath, Alan Moss, Brian Taylor, Alan Dixon …"

We leaned against the balcony rail, watching the five-a-side football.

"The thrill it was to walk into that cricket school. The musty smell of the dressing rooms. The little slope you walked up to go into the nets. The tiny bar where Alfred made tea and sandwiches. And all round the walls it was like a museum. Photographs of cricketers from all round the world. Plenty of Alf, of course."

172 East Hill, Wandsworth, South London. Every Saturday afternoon in winter from 1948.

"I remember the first ever lesson. I was in a group of fast bowlers, with Alan Moss, and we didn't get Alf. We got George Porter, a real Cockney lad. He was a Portsmouth football club fanatic. Always had to listen out for their result. Well, he watched us bowl a couple of balls each. Then he got us all together in a group. He said, 'I don't know how any of you got up here.' And just walked out. Left us to it. I think we all thought the same thing. 'We'll soon show him.' It was just his way of getting the best out of us."

I could see the improvement in my cricket. In 1993 I had taken 23 wickets at an average of 29.74; in 1994 it was 39 at 18.82.

The next winter's coaching did not start till January, with Ken mysteriously not answering his phone and never explaining why. It turned out later that he had had a minor stroke, affecting the vision in his left eye, but he wanted to carry on without our knowing that. We were glad to keep up the pretence.

The sessions were always fun, but we took them seriously. The batsmen would play themselves in properly, and the bowlers would discuss the weaknesses that they intended to probe. So good an atmosphere did Ken create that, on the one occasion he could not attend, we all turned up as usual and maintained the same environment.

After each session Ken was as eager as ever to stay and talk, and his mind would drift back to those early days at Alf Gover's.

"Once we'd had our lesson, we'd hang around in the hope that we could bowl at somebody else. There were four nets: with four batsmen and four coaches. We'd bowl at anybody and everybody. I remember once, when I was 17 or 18, I was bowling at this chap and he didn't look very good. There was a club cricketer in the next net, and I said to Alf, 'Excuse me, Mr Gover, do you think I could go and bowl at that feller next door?' 'All right, old boy.' Everybody was 'old boy' to Alfred. 'But what's the matter with this one?' 'Well, he isn't very good.' Isn't very good. Afterwards, he said to me, 'That's Peter May.' I don't know if Peter May heard. When I did play against him, he got 150 not out at Taunton."

Taunton. 7 June 1961
P.B.H. May not out 153
Biddulph 2 wickets for 84 runs

In the early days Alf was assisted by Andrew Sandham, scorer of 107 first-class centuries. "He was a real tough nut, the strictest of them all."

"Can I bowl in your net, please, Mr Sandham?"

"Yes, I should think so. As long as you can bowl half-volleys outside the off-stump. This young man's learning to play cover drives."

Ken was young and keen, but he let one drop down leg.

"How old are you?"

"I'm sixteen, Mr Sandham."

"Sixteen. I'm four times your age, and I can bowl better than that. Get out of my net."

Another coach was the Lancastrian Bill Lawton. "A funny man. He was going out with Dora Bryan. She used to come down to Alf's after theatre. I remember we were there one day; we were having our tea and sandwiches. And Lawty gets up. 'All right if I use t' phone, Alf?' And you couldn't help hearing the conversation. 'Can you tell me t' time of trains to Manchester? … Ay, that'll do.' He was going up about half past one, two o'clock in the morning. 'What are you going to Manchester for at that time of night?' we asked. 'Ee, I'm getting married in t' morning.' He was the most casual man you could come across. They're still married today."

Then Arthur Wellard arrived. The publican's son from South London, with his 'watcher, cock' manner. He had played his cricket for Somerset.

"We'd sit round the little wooden table with a pot of tea, and we'd listen to Arthur and Alf talking cricket. It was priceless. One of the highlights of the day. Not only did we look forward to our cricket lesson. We looked forward to the bit that came after."

Ken had grown up in Chingford, and he had watched his cricket at Lord's and The Oval – so he knew the players in Alf Gover's Surrey stories. But Arthur Wellard talked about Somerset: Bertie Buse and Mandy Mitchell-Innes, Harold Gimblett and Horace Hazell.

"Half of them I'd never heard of," Ken said. "I only saw them once, at Lord's, and I thought, 'My goodness, this is a funny sort of team.' Two players would chase the ball to the boundary. Then one would stop half-way and relay it back to the wicket-keeper."

Little could Ken have imagined then that he would finish up as part of this 'funny sort of team'.

"When I started down there, Ben Brocklehurst was the captain. 'We may not be the best batting side in the championship,' he said one day, 'but, when it comes to a swishing match, we're the best swishing side in the country.'"

I had just read David Foot's book, *Harold Gimblett – Tormented Genius of Cricket*, and I was fascinated by the batsman's mix of brilliance and mental torment, a torment that would eventually lead to his committing suicide.

"Gimblett was the senior professional when I went for my trial," Ken said. "I had to bowl at him in the nets."

"What was that like?"

"Interesting … Of course there were no tops to the nets, they couldn't afford anything like that, so I finished in the river a few times … But he was the one who got me my contract."

Ken was 21 years old, his national service over, and he dreamed of playing cricket for a living.

"The secretary called me in, offered me a six-month contract, starting at £30 a month. He said, 'How does that sound?' I was so excited about getting anything at all, but I thought, 'Six months, what happens after that?' I had a good job in the Borough Treasurer's Department in Chingford Town Hall. So I asked him, 'Could I have a little time to think about it?'"

Taunton, April 1954. Somerset versus Hampshire. A two-day friendly.

"I thought I'd go and ask Mr Gimblett. So I went along to the professionals' room, and I knocked on the door. 'Come in.' And Harold Gimblett was sitting there, all on his own. 'Come in, Greyhound,' he said. He called me the Greyhound. 'What can I do for you?'"

The game was starting. The umpires were out, the Hampshire team following. It was time for Harold to step out to open the innings.

"I wonder if I could have a word with you after close of play, Mr Gimblett."

"Never mind the close of play. Come in and sit down."

"But they'll be waiting for you."

"Never mind about them. They can wait."

Ken stood on the balcony of the Stratford Park Leisure Centre. As smart in his Somerset blazer as ever. There was a touch of the greyhound about him: the long face, the lean, bony body.

"Gimblett was a strange character."

"Let them wait," he said. "You're more important at the moment, Greyhound. What's on your mind?"

"I told him what the secretary had offered me."

We looked down on the five-a-side football, and he repeated the senior pro's advice.

"You can go back in and tell that stupid secretary of ours to shove it up his arse."

"I can't do that, Mr Gimblett."

"No, I suppose you can't. I'll tell him."

"Then I watched Harold Gimblett get 99 against Hampshire. He actually knocked Shack about the place, which was unusual. Then I went back to the secretary. 'What do you want?' he said. 'A two-year contract? Yes, certainly.'"

Back at 172, East Hill, Wandsworth, Alf was delighted. Another of his colts would be playing county cricket. "Congratulations, Old Boy."

"How did you get on at Somerset, cock?" Arthur asked.

"Not too bad, Mr Wellard. I got a two-year contract."

"You? Given you a contract? Oh well, I suppose they're glad to get hold of anybody down there."

Down to size before he had even started.

"If it hadn't have been for cricket," Ken reflected, "I'd have finished up a wizened old stick in Chingford Town Hall."

"How long were you at Somerset with Harold Gimblett then, Ken?"

"I wound up my job and went back down a week or two later. They were playing Yorkshire, I remember. I went down to the ground nice and early to bowl in the nets. Half past nine, maybe. And walking through the main gates in St James Street, I bumped into Harold Gimblett. All these small boys came running up for his autograph. So he was signing away, and I was standing to one side, waiting. Then they turned to me. 'Can we have yours?' 'Oh no,' I said, 'you don't want mine.' And I started to walk through the gates. It was the first time anybody had asked for my autograph."

The young boys at Stroud ran past him now without a second look.

"Gimblett didn't half give me a bollocking."

"You sign. You sign those autographs. Don't you ever refuse a boy an autograph."

"But they don't even know who I am. They've never seen me play."

"Yes, and by this time next week they will have seen you play. And they probably won't want your autograph."

Gimblett and Wellard. Their cricketing glory had been fifty or sixty years earlier; their world had long passed. Yet here I was, standing with somebody who was speaking of them with such freshness that I could almost touch them. I could certainly hear them.

"Did Arthur Wellard ever tell you the story of Harold Gimblett's debut? He played in that match, didn't he?"

"He was batting at the other end."

We were back in the Wandsworth cricket school. Alf was pouring out the tea, and Ken and his fellow colts were pulling up their wooden chairs.

"We were goin' to Frome to play Essex," Arthur started. "And we only 'ad ten of us who were qualified to play. And somebody said, 'Who was that young lad in the nets the other day? 'E's Somerset born.'"

It was May 1935. Harold Gimblett was a 20-year-old farmer's boy, on a fortnight's trial at the County Ground, and he had made no impression in the nets. For the last few days of his trial he had been put to helping the groundsman. He could have scored three thousand runs a summer thereafter, back at his club in Watchet, and they would always have said, 'Just a farmer's boy. We had a look at him, and he was nothing.'

That Saturday morning, according to David Foot's book, the young Harold left home at six o'clock. He carried his bag across muddy farm fields, only to see his bus pulling away down the lane. The next one was two hours away. He thumbed down a lorry, and the driver asked him where he was going. To Frome, to play cricket. For Somerset. Would you believe him?

"Go on, Arthur. Tell us what happened."

"'E arrived in the dressin' room," Arthur went on. "'E'd got a bat that looked as if it had been knocked together by a couple of nails. 'You're not goin' out to bat with that, are you, son?' I said. 'Go and 'ave a look in my bag. There's a bat in there.'"

The late call-up. The missed bus. The borrowed bat. It was a lovely story.

Arthur took a sip of tea.

"I was battin' when 'e came in. We were in terrible trouble, weren't we? We were six down, and we couldn't 'ave 'ad more than about a hundred. 'All right, son,' I said. 'I'll look after Nick.'"

"Nick?" I asked.

"That was Morris Nichols," Ken explained. "He was quick."

"I'll take Nick. See 'ow you get on at the other end."

"And who was on at the other end, Ken?"

"Peter Smith. Bowling leg-breaks and googlies."

"See 'ow you get on at the other end. I don't reckon 'Arold knew a leg break from a googly, but 'e sorted him out. Kept 'ittin' 'im out of the ground, didn't 'e?"

The Frome scoreboard only displayed the total, not the individual scores, but in little more than an hour the young Harold completed the fastest century of 1935. He went on to make more than 23,000 first-class runs. The highest run-scorer in Somerset's history.

Arthur Wellard played cricket for Somerset from 1927 to 1950. He took 1,614 wickets and scored 12,485 runs. A big man, he hit over a quarter of all his runs in sixes. Twice he hit five consecutively, but that afternoon at Frome he was no match for the farmer's boy from Bicknoller.

"I always remember the way he told the story," Ken told me.

"I was on seven when 'e came in to bat. Ten minutes later I'm still stuck on seven, and 'e's got 30. And I was the 'itter."

Twenty years had passed between the innings and this story round Alf's little wooden table. Another forty before Ken drew back from the balcony and told me.

"I loved the way he put it. 'And I was the 'itter.' Priceless."

Ken did not play in the match against Yorkshire. He was a youngster, starting out on his life of cricket, happy to bowl in the nets at the first team. But Gimblett was the batsman they all looked to for entertainment and for runs, and he did not cope with the pace of a raw Fred Trueman.

Taunton. 12, 13, 14 May 1954

H. Gimblett c Lister b Trueman 0   lbw b Trueman 5

"I never saw him again. He just packed his bags at the end of the match and went."

Harold Gimblett. 50 first-class centuries and three Tests for England.

The story of his debut is full of light and joy, but a darker world had taken over. The farmer's boy had become the nerve-wracked senior professional. The previous winter he had undergone electro-convulsive therapy at Tone Vale mental hospital.

"I think he carried the Somerset batting for years, you know. Roy Smith tells the story of how he opened with him against Worcester once."

Roy Smith: 96 matches for Somerset, one century.

"Reg Perks was seaming and swinging the ball all over the place. And Roy couldn't get a bat on it. Gimblett came down the wicket. 'Come here, son. Are you having a bit of a problem down there? ... I'll tell you what. I'll look after Perksy for a few overs. You come down this end.' Then, after Gimblett had hit him for three or four fours, he said, 'There you are, son. He might be a bit easier for you now.'"

Frome. 27 June 1953

R. Smith c Broadbent b Flavell 100

Harold Gimblett. In March 1978 he took an overdose of tablets and died.

"Perhaps he was a lot better player than he thought. Tony Hancock never thought he was a very good comedian, did he?"

Ken had this reflective side, but he preferred not to stay serious for too long.

"I bought a new bat at the start of 1961," he said, switching the subject. "Took it out for a net, and Bill Alley bowled this ball at me. I played it back. 'Here, what's that bat you've got down there?' He banged a ball up and down on it. 'That's much too good for you. I'll give you one of mine.' And he went out that summer and scored 3,000 runs with my bat. You can see it in the museum at Taunton."

So who was the last man to buy a bat that scored 3,000 first-class runs in a season? Answer, Ken Biddulph.

Part of the charm of listening to Ken was that he never spoke as if he had been much of a cricketer so it was easy to identify with his stories. Yet in his best summer, 1960, he had taken 83 wickets.

My own game continued to improve under Ken's guidance. "Now then, young man,' he said to me the next autumn. 'How many wickets did you take last summer?"

"Fifty."

"Well, aim for sixty this year."

"Oh, I don't know about that, Ken. I'm 47 years old now, you know."

"47, that's nothing. When I was 47, I won the Bowling Award in the Durham League."

The summer of 1996 was my best ever season. I averaged over 30 with the bat, and I took 82 wickets.

"Come on now, Shack, keep those arms up high. Let's see you attack the crease."

Through his early Somerset years Ken returned each Saturday in winter to Alf Gover's, and he sat with his fellow colts around the pot of tea.

"What do you think of Lindwall, Alfred? They're calling him the Peter Pan of fast bowlers."

"Peter Pan," Alf snorted. "I was still bowling fast at 40. He's only 34. I had a phone call from Wally Hammond, you know. 'Alf,' he said. 'We'd like you to play in the next Test match.' 'I'm forty years old now, Wally.' 'I know, Alf, but you're still the quickest in the country.'"

"But Lindwall's a pretty good bowler, though, Alf?"

"Well, he was all right after I showed him how to bowl the other one."

The next week it was Arthur Wellard at the table.

"What do you think of Ray Lindwall, Arthur?"

"Ray Lindwall?" he said. "'E was nothing special till I showed 'im 'ow to bowl the other one."

Ken returned to his car, and I helped him with all his paraphernalia. His two bats, one with the sides shaved away. The length of string for demonstrating bowling lines. The pair of artificial wickets. A small bowling machine, with an extension lead. And the balls: tennis balls, twin-coloured balls, junior balls and the box of specials.

"I remember at Somerset, going along to the office to get a ball at the beginning of my time there, and I had to sign for it. And it wasn't a new ball, either. That was my ball, I was responsible for it. I'd take it home and polish it up every evening."

He locked the boot and continued

"By the middle of July it was getting a bit tatty. So I went to see if there was any chance of another ball. 'Another?' he said. 'What have you been doing to it? You've only had that this summer.'"

The wind in the car park blew through his silver grey hair.

"Arthur offered me his cricket bag, you know. It was one of those lovely old leather bags. But I said no. I went and bought a canvas one. I didn't want a second-hand bag. I was young. I didn't realise. Just imagine. I could have played my career with Arthur Wellard's bag."

He opened his car door. Half his mind on the journey home, the other half back around that little wooden table in Alf Gover's School.

"I loved the way he put it. 'And I was the 'itter.' Priceless. See you next Friday, young man."

Dear Ken. I can still hear him saying it.

"See you next Friday, young man."

In July 1996 I played in Ken's last cricket match. At Sheepscombe. On the Laurie Lee field, a plateau above the village.

We had played there the previous year. Ken Biddulph's XI. We were all people he had been coaching that winter, and he sent Alistair and me out to open the innings with strict instructions to play ourselves in … bat properly … don't throw it away … plenty of time. The next batsmen all got the same advice, and at tea we had reached about 120 for three.

I don't think Ken had ever played this sort of village cricket, where you bat to tea, then the other team bats. So I could see trouble brewing when he told me at the table that he thought things were going well and that we should be able to declare just before six o'clock. Out of the corner of my eye I saw the Sheepscombe captain Piers Risely-Pritchard, an irascible character who had once been on the books at Hampshire, appearing from his dressing room with his pads on.

A minute or two later the fun started.

"Oh," Ken said with surprise. "I didn't say I'd declared, did I?"

"You've got to be joking. We've been bowling in that heat since half past two. You can't be serious."

But Ken got his way. Not that it did us much good. The Sheepscombe captain was in such a stew by six o'clock that he smacked our bowling everywhere.

The game the following summer, Ken's last, became an all-day one – though we spent so long in the Butcher's Arms at lunchtime that I'm not sure we played any more cricket.

In mid-afternoon Ken bowled three overs, and at the age of 64 he still moved the ball both ways off the seam. A chance flew through the slips, then my friend Humphrey dived forward at extra cover and got the name of Biddulph once more among the wickets. "It was a good catch, that," Ken said, but his own drop at mid-off preyed on him and he decided to call it a day. "I've lost some vision on this left side," he explained.

Ken had been a Somerset cricketer for eight golden years. He had played 91 matches, taken 270 wickets and could talk with insight and humour about almost every cricketer of his day. I never grew tired of his company.

I think he was glad of my company, too. "The mind conjures up memories," he said one day, "and that's something you can't buy."

When the 1997 *Wisden* appeared, its Births and Deaths of Cricketers had been reorganised. The qualification for inclusion had gone up from 50 matches to 100, and the list now jumped from Bicknell to Bilby. Ken was a forgotten man, and it set him off on another story.

"I'd had a winter job in the local sports shop. George Hinton and Sons. Almost next to the Berni Inn Steak Bar in the centre of Taunton. I used to take a van out, go round the clubs, pubs, factories, schools, flog them sports kit. The shop had a great big picture of me in the window, a life-size cardboard cut-out of me bowling."

Then in August 1961 the Somerset committee decided not to offer him another contract. "The next time I walked past the shop, I looked in the window and my picture had gone."

That winter the netting at Stratford Park came away from its runners, and nobody repaired it. "They're hopeless here," Ken said. With Alistair and Ed now at work, unable to get away on a Friday afternoon, our sessions lost much of their excellence.

Early the following summer, making a mess of a catch, I sustained a hairline fracture of my left thumb. Three days later, ignoring the pain, I played again, and I dropped another catch. This one left my thumb, in the surgeon's words, "smashed to smithereens". It was rebuilt under general anaesthetic, and I walked around for weeks with a great staple-like contraption sticking through it. At the end of the summer I had taken just 14 wickets.

By then my life had moved into a new phase, and it all flowed from the hours I had spent with Ken on the balcony at Stratford Park Leisure Centre.

In the autumn of 1996 I attended an evening class in Feature Writing at Bath University. I had always wanted to write, and in my desk drawer were a few semi-autobiographical short stories that I would get out from time to time. But this course, with its focus on journalism rather than literature, was just what I needed. It shook the introspectiveness out of my writing.

In one of the later weeks our tutor Hazel gave us a long talk, about how we had to find our own specialist subjects to cultivate, and my mind wandered for a while. What about Ken Biddulph, I thought? All those wonderful stories he tells, how can I make something from them? I know, I'll get him to talk about his most memorable match.

A week later Ken and I were sitting in The Old Fleece Inn, just south of Stroud. He had run a public house for a while in the north-east, and he was rarely impressed when we visited such establishments: either the beer was not good or the landlord was unnecessarily miserable. So we had already put our heads in two other places before as a last resort we settled on the spit-and-sawdust of The Old Fleece. I balanced my tape recorder between us on the rickety wooden table, and Ken was away.

"I'm going to choose Yorkshire at Bath in '59, towards the end of the season. The reason I pick that one is that in those days it was a great achievement to beat Yorkshire. It's the only occasion I was on the winning side against them. I don't remember getting more than a couple of wickets in the first innings, but I do remember getting Brian Close caught at slip for 128. Is that right?"

I had found the page in the pile of *Wisdens* that I had brought with me.

"Yes, that's right."

"I still reckon he was a good one to get out, even though he did have a hundred. He was always looking to get after you. One thing I did learn was, I never bowled at his legs."

"Did he achieve everything he could have done in his career?"

"Closey? Funny man, Closey. He could be both a brilliant genius and thick at the same time. If you played against Closey, you'd know you were going to have a tough game. A great opponent … The thing about Closey is that, if you listened to him, he was never wrong. You tended to get into the habit of believing everything he said was right."

In the background of the tape there is the sound of a fruit machine spilling out its winnings while Ken starts to recall how for that match he stayed at the Francis Hotel in Bath's Queen's Square.

"Colin McCool was my room-mate. He was a great cricketer, came over here with Bradman's Australians in '48, and he would tell me lots of stories about Bradman. He worshipped him. He modelled his own batting on Bradman. In fact, he roomed with Bradman on that tour. So there I was in the Francis Hotel. What an honour! I was sharing a room with a bloke who'd shared a room with Don Bradman.

"He wrote a book, Colin. Called it *Cricket Is A Game*. He kept me awake half the night through, practically the whole season, with his typewriter. Two o'clock in the morning I'd wake up. Clink-a-clink-clink. 'Colin, what are you doing?' 'Get back to sleep,' he'd say. 'I'm writing a book.'"

The match at Bath came down to the last afternoon when Yorkshire, top of the table and pressing for their first championship for ten years, were chasing 255 to win.

"Yorkshire were a hard team to play. The atmosphere was always a little bit different. They had this self-belief. They could not be beaten. When you went in to bat against Yorkshire, they used to look at your boots, as if to say, 'What are you doing? How dare you come out here?' That was the impression. You felt very much unwanted."

Bath was a council-owned ground, with little cricket played there besides the county's four games, and it had a reputation for taking turn. Brian Langford was Somerset's off-spinner – "Langy always did well at Bath" – and he took six Yorkshire wickets as, in a thrilling finish, Somerset triumphed by 16 runs. It was their first victory over the Northerners since 1903 – and during the match Ken was awarded his county cap.

"I had to buy a couple of bottles of champagne to go round the dressing room. Invite the visiting team in for a quick glass of bubbly. And I remember I couldn't afford it. I had to get it on credit from Bill Moor the caterer. I think it took me about a month to pay for it."

After the match was over, Ken said, some of the Yorkshire team stayed for drinks. "Closey was one of them. We sat listening to him for half an hour. How it would have been different if Fred Trueman hadn't been away at the Test match. How they should have lapped Brian Langford. How the game was there for the taking. We'd beaten Yorkshire for the first time for 56 years, I'd been awarded my county cap but, after half an hour of listening to Closey, we thought we were the ones who'd lost. They could not be beaten."

The next day I visited the public library in Bath and found a report of the game in *The Times*.

> *When Close arrived, his approach, his immense skill, which was evident from the beginning, and some Somerset bowling far short of the standard required, enabled Yorkshire to prosper … Then Langford began spinning to his heart's content.*

The game ran through my veins: the twists and turns that characterise cricket at its best, the players that Ken had brought alive, the moments of personal drama. And I couldn't help looking at the stories on the other pages of the paper: the M1 running to Rugby, soon to be extended to Doncaster; the battle between Debenham's and the House of Fraser for control of Harrod's; the advertisement for *Phosdrin*, an organo-phosphorus insecticide with 'dramatic killing power'.

"You've got to hear a voice reading it," our tutor Hazel had said. "You've got to catch a rhythm." I worked for hours to weave together the various strands: the *Times* report, the titbits of contemporary life and, above all, Ken's voice. "You've got to go on and on editing it until it sounds right."

Eventually it did sound right. I had found a style that seemed to work. Present tense, cultural context and the warm glow of happy memories.

I sent it to Ken. "You *have* been working hard," he said at our next net. "You know more about the game than I do." And he was away again, about what 'Locky' and Alec Bedser said to him the next day and the time he met Harold Macmillan at a charity match at Haywards Heath. "I sat next to him at tea. I was dying to know what it was like to be a prime minister. He didn't want to know, though. All he wanted to do was to talk cricket. He wanted to know what it was like being a professional cricketer."

I found a scorecard of a 1955 charity match, in which Macmillan had played. Hit wicket bowled Hearne, 2. The Hearne in question was Richard, television's Mister Pastry. I added that to the piece.

I started to wonder. Could I get some other cricketers to talk to me? Maybe I could even make a book out of it all.

"Who could I interview from the other counties?" I asked Ken, and he suggested Martin Horton. So I wrote to Mr M. Horton in Worcester, enclosing a copy of Ken's game, and I waited anxiously for a reply.

"I should be delighted to help in any way I can," he wrote back. "I'd also like to choose a game when we beat Yorkshire. Would that be all right?"

After Martin came Arthur Milton in Bristol. "We had a very good game at Cheltenham once. Against Yorkshire. We beat them."

I sat on his sofa, with my cup of tea, and I thought for a moment. Shall I make that the book? *The Day We Beat Yorkshire.* It seemed it was every cricketer's favourite memory.

I travelled all over England and Wales, interviewing former cricketers, and the result was a twelve-chapter book, which I called *Runs in the Memory.* I could not find a publisher for it; they all said it lacked commercial potential. They didn't want Ken Biddulph and Martin Horton; they wanted Freddie Trueman and Colin Cowdrey. So I published it myself – as Fairfield Books. It came out in October 1997.

I dedicated it to Ken, and I gave him the first copy. For once he was lost for words.

That first book seemed to touch a nerve among a generation of older readers, and I wrote a sequel on the 1960s. From those beginnings I turned gradually into a full-time writer and publisher, a sort of oral historian of cricket. To date it has given me fourteen years of pleasure, and none of it would have happened if it had not been for Ken.

More importantly, I am still playing cricket each summer, seventeen years on from that first coaching session. What was it he said? "If I can get you a few more runs, a few more wickets, keep you enjoying the game for a few more years, you'll be happy, won't you?"

Each spring Ken organised a weekend coaching course. He advertised it in the *Cricketer* magazine, and a dozen or so club cricketers from all around England would enrol, staying two nights at a guest house on the outskirts of Cheltenham. Once our Friday afternoons at Stratford Park had fizzled out, I took to joining them for some of the sessions.

It was an eye-opener to see how anxious Ken became with a group of strangers: anxious to make sure that everybody was happy, that it all went smoothly, that they were getting value for money. He took great trouble over all the arrangements, laying on guest speakers and plenty of food and drink.

One year he took us for Saturday lunch at a country pub. It was the height of the BSE crisis, and he had ordered minced beef all round. Next to me was a charming Anglicised Indian called Francis, an accountancy lecturer.

"I'm not sure I want to eat beef at the moment," he said to me.

"I agree," I said.

"Excuse me," he called across to the waitress. "Would you mind if I don't have the beef?"

She was most understanding, offering him an omelette. So I joined in. "Could I have one too?" I asked, and her can't-do-enough-to-help charm turned in an instant to angry shouting: "Don't be such a bloody nuisance. He's got his religious reasons. You're just causing trouble."

After she had left the room, Francis turned to me with a grin. "I hit the four," he said, "and you got the bouncer next ball."

It would have been very funny – if I had not glanced down the table and spotted the look of horrified alarm on Ken's face.

Ken turned seventy in May 2002, and I made him a card. I had been through my *Wisdens*, finding all the times he had dismissed great batsmen cheaply, and I arranged ten of them into a pretend scorecard: Cowdrey b Biddulph 6, Graveney c & b Biddulph 7, May c Atkinson b Biddulph 5 and, of course, Marshall c Lomax b Biddulph 0. It added up to 67, and I headed it 'BATTING GREATS CRASH TO 67 ALL OUT – BIDDULPH TAKES ALL TEN'. Inside I wrote, 'K.D. Biddulph, not out 70.'

He rang as soon as he had read it, purring with pleasure and reliving every wicket in detail. "I'm going to take it up to Gloucester to show Bomber Wells," he said. Then the tone of triumph disappeared out of his voice. "I know what will happen. He'll read the names, and he'll say, 'I got every one of those first ball.'"

By this time I was writing articles for *Wisden Cricket Monthly*, and I often drew on Ken as a source, meeting him for lunch at a pub, usually The Cross Hands on the A46. On one occasion, when I was writing about the work cricketers did in winter, I got him to reminisce about the time he and Malcolm Heath spent on Stuart Surridge's willow plantations.

"We used a cross-cut saw to fell the trees, then we had to chop them into rounds with axes. The second winter they produced one of these petrol-driven chain-saws, but only the pros were allowed to use it. We had to carry it for them, and even that was hard work. Much heavier than they are today. We stayed on a farm where we were fed on good home-grown food: steak every night, and lashings of egg and bacon for breakfast."

The publican interrupted with our sandwiches, resisting Ken's attempt to draw him into a cheery exchange. "He's not exactly mine host, is he?" Ken said after he'd left our table. "The way he's going on, this pub isn't going to last long."

Then he was back in the 1950s: "The farmer had a deaf father. Every evening, when *The Archers* was on, he used to press his ear against this blaring radio. And he could sit in any part of the room and spit with alarming accuracy into the fire.

"That tree felling job, it was the best thing that ever happened to me. It made me very fit and strong. After that I never once had a problem with my back, not even bowling on that concrete thing at Taunton. All that hard work, all that good food, at the end of the day a couple of pints of good old English ale, that's what you need to be a good fast bowler."

But Ken, being Ken, could not resist ending his speech with a putdown.

"It's a pity I didn't become a good fast bowler."

He told me of his plan to write a book about his years in cricket. I recall his words when we parted that day: "You always get me remembering so much. I'm going to cut down on the coaching and get going on that book."

He died of a heart attack the following January. He had been rushing about, worrying as always about everybody else: his wife in hospital, his mother in care, a coaching group he did not want to let down.

His daughter Kim rang. "I was wondering if I could possibly ask you something," she said. "Do say no if you don't want to. I'll quite understand.

But would you be prepared to say a few words at the funeral? He always spoke so much about your writing."

It was funny. Ken had never really told me he liked my writing.

The church was at the top of a hill near Minchinhampton Common, and the pews were crowded by the time the service started. The last to arrive, escorted slowly to the front, was his mother. We began by singing *All Things Bright and Beautiful*, though the tune was completely unfamiliar to me and, by the sound of it, to most of the congregation.

> *The cold wind in the winter,*
> *The pleasant summer sun,*
> *The ripe fruits in the garden,*
> *He made them every one.*

We murmured along as best we could, and after some prayers and a psalm I gave my address. I told the story of how I had come to know Ken – "Good news, Stephen. There's nobody in after us till six o'clock" – and they all laughed. Then they laughed some more as I repeated the stories he had told me, back on that balcony at the leisure centre.

"I've come all the way from Southampton to see Marshall bat, and some stupid bugger's got him out … And, when they have seen you play, I don't suppose they'll want your autograph … Bloody fools, we could be halfway back to Taunton by now."

From the lectern I could see the glowing faces: Alistair from the nets, Malcolm Heath, Bomber Wells, Bill Alley, Tom Graveney. Once again Ken had got them all laughing.

Seven years have passed since that funeral, and I can still hear Ken's voice, just as he could hear that of his mentor Alf Gover in Wandsworth fifty years earlier: "By the way, old boy, the batsman you didn't want to bowl at, his name's Peter May." And that of Arthur Wellard, reaching back a further generation to the Gimblett century at Frome: "You're not goin' out to bat with that, are you, son? Go and 'ave a look in my bag."

The voices will echo down the generations, as long as there are story tellers to pass them on. Ken may not have been the greatest of cricketers, but he was a great coach and a great story teller.

That half hour I asked him for, all those years ago, it's not over yet.

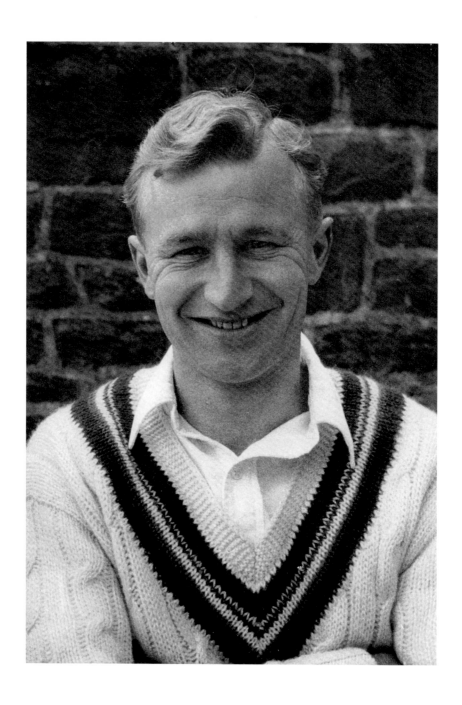

2

ARTHUR MILTON

A life turned round

Clement Arthur Milton

Born: Bristol, 10 March 1928

Died: Bristol, 25 April 2007

Back in 1982 Frank Keating wrote a portrait of Arthur Milton in *The Guardian*. 'No paradise lost for this Milton' was the headline. Accompanying it was a photograph of the former footballing cricketer on a Post Office bicycle, delivering the mail around the streets of north Bristol.

> 'He is in the sorting office by ten past five, gets his bundle into street order, then whistles off to the Downs of Clifton in cycle-clips … and no, he doesn't think much, anymore, of his previous incarnation on the foreign fields of fame.'

I can't remember if I bought *The Guardian* that day or if somebody cut out the piece for me, but I kept it in a drawer. It is rare for a newspaper article to stay with me much beyond the day, but this one never left my imagination.

So fifteen years later, after I had written two chapters of my book, with Ken Biddulph and Martin Horton, I found myself wondering if I could track down Arthur Milton.

I found his number in the Bristol telephone directory: Milton, C.A. and an address in Henleaze. I had not picked up the phone like this before; it seemed intrusive. But I made myself do it, and he agreed without fuss to see me. We settled on Monday of the following week.

"What time would you like to come?" he asked in a gentle Bristol accent.

"I'll come early if you like. Say nine o'clock."

"Oh no, no, don't come that early. I've got three paper rounds to get done."

Forty-five years earlier, when *The Times* newspaper ran to only ten pages and sport filled just one of them, he had run out of the tunnel at Wembley Stadium, to play for England against Austria. A young, fair-haired winger whose only league football had been twelve appearances for Arsenal. *The Times* report filled one of the seven columns on the page. 'Milton did two or three things in the game to show his undoubted quality,' it read, 'but the occasion and tension generally were too much for him.'

Seven years later, with *The Times* now up to sixteen pages, he had walked out of the pavilion at Headingley, opening the batting for England against New Zealand and scoring a century on debut. 'The impression one gained was of a player with a first-rate temperament and a placid disposition. He has the look of one of Nature's games players.'

By January 1997, when I nervously rang him, he was the only man living in England who had played both football and cricket for his country, the last in that special line of double internationals. Yet at the age of 68 he was leaving home before sunrise on cold winter mornings, clambering onto his old Post Office bicycle and enduring the biting winds, the rain and the sleet to deliver newspapers to the houses around the Bristol Downs. Some of them were great chunky newspapers, too, and he had to separate their sections to get them through the letter boxes.

"I collect the money on a Monday," he told me when I arrived. "Cote Paddock, where I finish up, used to be on my old Post Office round. There are bungalows and flats there, mostly old ladies, and they're very punctual. They've always got the money out ready for you. I give them a bit of time. They've all got their marbles, and some of them are very interesting. They've had interesting lives. And they don't see many people; they're on their own mostly."

Arthur Milton had played football for England at Wembley, in front of 100,000 people, and he possessed a medal as part of Arsenal's championship winning side of 1952/53. He had opened the batting for England at Lord's, and he was second only to the great Wally Hammond among Gloucestershire's run-scorers. One of Nature's games players.

Yet here I was, agreeing to see him after lunch because he had three paper rounds to complete and because he liked to stop and listen to the lives of the old ladies.

He rode a bicycle that he had kept after ten years of working as a postman. "I've got two actually. The ladies' ones are the best, because you can get your legs through easy. The old Post Office bikes are good; they look after the weight of the papers."

We got down to business in his front room, talking about his most memorable game of cricket, and I did not pursue the conversation about the paper round. But it stayed with me. It haunted me, and over the following years I revisited him from time to time, fascinated by the course his life had taken and by the contentment he seemed to have found.

Back in 1946, an eighteen-year-old at Cotham Grammar, he had sent for the entry forms to study mathematics at Oxford University. Then the mighty Arsenal arrived, and he signed their forms instead, starting out on a career of almost thirty years as a professional sportsman. He had been a hero to many on the terraces and around the boundaries, a good-looking young man with a natural balance about everything he did. Yet, as I was to discover, he was less at ease with his life as a sportsman than he was on his bicycle pedalling uphill to the Downs.

"It's good exercise. It keeps me fit. You have no idea of the gradients till you ride a bike. And it's magical up there. There's always early moisture in the grass and, when the old sun comes up over the horizon, she lifts the moisture into a mist that runs across the Downs. Then she'll get up a bit higher and move it all. Spring and autumn are best."

His voice had an easy drawl, never hurried, lingering philosophically over the words. "I love it. I shall go on doing it as long as I can."

He had given some thought to his choice of memorable match. He started by telling me about Bomber Wells' debut, how this unlikely character from the back streets of Gloucester arrived in their dressing room one morning, taking the place of the great off-spinner Tom Goddard. "We'd never seen him before. He just strolled in, changed, came out; nothing seemed to worry him at all. And he kept getting people out. He took six wickets in the Sussex first innings. He just bowled off one or two paces, and you didn't realise straightaway, he was so strong that the ball used to pitch much further up to you than you thought. And every now and then he'd bowl a leg break. It was incredible how he did it. The ball used to go up in the air, and of course nobody had ever seen anything like it before."

Then he mentioned two more games. One was at Bristol against Kent – "This is very immodest of me," is all he said – and one at Leyton against Essex which ended in a tie in the last possible over.

"I like the sound of that," I said decisively so I never got to hear about the Kent match.

For almost two hours he talked: about the game at Leyton, about the skills and the personalities of the players in the two sides, about the way of life of the county cricketer in those days and, from time to time, about his thoughts on sport and its proper place in our lives. The conversation meandered gently, and a chapter started to form in my head.

"I was captain for the match. I said to Doug Insole, 'You declare now. We'll go all the way through. We won't block out. We'll have a result.' … Cooky, he wasn't the worst with the bat. He made a hundred when he was in the 'raf', you know, at a place called Bulawayo. He always used to talk about his hundred at Bulawayo. … Up and down the A4. We knew every fish and chip shop on that road. … It was three to win, and Trevor bowled a wide. It swung a lot, see. You should have seen the look on his face. He could have cut his throat, couldn't he? … I'd have stayed with my mother-in-law in Muswell Hill, saved the three-pound-a-night lodging money. That was quite a bit of bunce. … Trevor was a great bowler. If you're going to be an all-rounder for England, you've got to be good enough at one of them. And Trevor was. … Barrie Meyer, he hits the ball down to third man, and he's looking for two to win the game. … I think the Leyton ground was owned by the council. The outfield was very rough. … He said afterwards, 'I should have gone for it. The odds were in my favour.' … Then Cooky was back on strike, and he got caught at short leg off the glove. … It was the only tie I played in. … They were wonderful days in the sun. The days were never long enough. … These days it all revolves around money, see. It puts too much pressure on to win, and I don't think that's good. But that's the way of the world now."

Then he stopped. "That's enough about me," he said. "What about you? You say you're not working at the college now."

As I was saying goodbye at the front door, he returned briefly to the cricket. "You can read about that other game. We played Kent at Bristol. One of the years Tom Pugh was captain. I'll leave you to look it up."

Back home I annotated the tape. I loved his description of Sam Cook at Lord's, batting with 'old Tom Goddard': "It was a bloody pantomime. Goddard was always trying to be in charge, he was about six foot three. Sam calls him for a run, gets half way up the wicket and sees he's got no chance. So he turns and beats Tom back to the other end. You should have heard them when they came in."

And I loved his story of Richard Bernard, a Cambridge undergraduate who had joined the team in the summer of that Leyton game. In his first match, against the mighty Surrey at The Oval, he had been put down to bat at number seven, and in each innings he had gone to the wicket at 31 for five.

"We were back at Bristol for the next match, playing Northants, I think it was, and somebody said, 'Don't worry, Richie, it won't be as bad this time.' Well, he went in at 16 for five."

This was what I wanted to write about, the fun of cricket. Wonderful days in the sun, days that were never long enough. So I didn't make much of the passages on the tape when he talked about the captaincy problems they had at Gloucestershire or how he didn't feel at home when he played in the England team. Nor did I linger long on his thoughts about professional sport, how it's better to have a proper job and to play your sport part-time. These things lodged in my consciousness, but it was some time before I would explore them.

I did look up the game against Kent at Bristol. It was August 1962. In the first innings he made 110 not out. Then, in the second, when Gloucestershire needed one run for victory with one ball remaining, he was on strike, 98 not out. According to one newspaper, 'he stepped out of his crease to make a sparkling on-drive to the boundary.'

He never mentioned it again.

Some time after I finished the chapter, I met up with Richard Bernard, the Cambridge undergraduate. He had become a general practitioner in Downend, just as his great-great-uncle W.G. Grace had been, and he invited me to lunch.

His cricket for Gloucestershire amounted to only a handful of games so his memory of the time was uncluttered. At Leyton Doug Insole, a leg-sided batsman, had hit a big hundred, and Richard recalled how hopeless he had felt when bowling at him. Anything on off stump went through mid-on, middle stump through mid-wicket and, if he bowled wide of off, he got cut.

"How do I bowl at him, Milt?" he asked his skipper in desperation. "He plays so wrongly." And back came the brisk response: "Just bowl straight and bowl a length."

"I got on very well with Arthur, but his reply made me very discouraged."

He then related a tale from a game two weeks later at Dover, when he found himself dropped to twelfth man. For the matches at Bristol the drinks and the errands were all handled by the team's masseur, Harry White, and it did not occur to him that it might be different when they were away.

"I spent the first morning in the scorer's box. Dover is a beautiful ground, with these tiers of banking, and I enjoyed myself greatly. Then, when I went to lunch, I had a terrible mauling from Arthur: 'Where were you? We were wanting drinks. We were wanting sweaters.' He was furious. 'I'm terribly sorry,' I said. 'I had no idea. I'm very new on this.' I was so abject in my apology, he finished up apologising to me."

It was another Arthur, not the mellow, contented man with the newspaper rounds, talking of wonderful days in the sun.

I wrote a book with Bomber Wells, centred on a game at Cheltenham, and Arthur contributed some memories to that.

"We used to lunch with the Mayor on the first day. There was one occasion in my early days when George Lambert and Colin Scott were playing. We had some wine, and I think George had one or two glasses too many. He came up to bowl the first over after lunch, and he ran straight into the wickets."

Bomber told me what I had by then heard from so many sources. Arthur was a natural at any game: cricket, football, golf, lawn tennis, even picking winners at the greyhound track. "Every game he played he'd beat you. Darts, billiards, snooker, table tennis. He had this little rubber ball in his bag. We had to bounce it across the table. The trick was to get it to nick the edge. You'd play up to five or ten. He was even unbeatable at that."

Tom Cartwright of Warwickshire remembered a match against Gloucestershire at Coventry. "The midlands snooker champion was there. He wanted to know if anybody wanted to play him. Nobody in our dressing room would do it so we went into the Gloucestershire dressing room and they all said, 'Get Arthur.' And Arthur beat him."

Everything he did had stardust sprinkled over it. Yet there remained a feeling that he could have achieved more. "He never used half his talent, but the half he used was marvellous," was what Bomber said. Tom Graveney put it slightly differently: "If Arthur had had a little bit of devilment in him, he would have been a hell of a cricketer."

A natural games player. Perhaps, I found myself wondering, it all came too naturally. He had never had to work at it.

Bomber, when he was in an uncharitable mood, would call him lazy, even suggesting that Arthur had let himself down by becoming a postman – though, more often, he would look at that from the other direction: "Milt could have had any job in the country with his sporting pedigree, but he became a postman. And when he wasn't delivering letters, he was decorating or doing the old pensioners' gardens. He never, ever forgot his roots."

It reminded me of what Arthur had said about his tour of Australia, the ill-fated trip in 1958/59 when Peter May's much-trumpeted team had lost 4-0: "It wasn't my scene. It was still the days of the amateurs: May, Cowdrey, Bailey. I wasn't impressed with Peter May as captain. He was a very nice chap, but he was aloof; he didn't take enough interest in the people in the team. He was probably shy. At the end of it I was pleased to get back to my own tump, to my own pals who I knew how to play with. I was happy there."

It reminded me, too, of his one football international. On the right wing for Arsenal he had formed a brilliant partnership with the Scottish inside forward Jimmy Logie, but that afternoon at Wembley he achieved no such rapport with Ivor Broadis of Manchester City. Indeed, for long periods of play, he stayed out on the wing, waiting in vain to be brought into the action. "I should have gone and looked for the ball a bit more," he said. "I didn't have a good game. Really I'd have liked Jim to come along and play with me."

Yet his debut in Test cricket was a great success: an unbeaten century, the first England player to remain on the field throughout a Test match. "Your first game, it sharpens your concentration a bit," he explained. "I did need a kick up the backside."

Were these just the explanations of the older man, trying to put the successes and failures of his youth into neatly labelled boxes? Or had he reached another level with it all? He continued to fascinate me.

Cricket captaincy clearly interested him. "George Emmett was the best I played under," he said emphatically, a view I heard often among that generation of Gloucestershire cricketers. "David Allen was good, too, when he did it. I could have played under him."

"I liked Doug Insole," he said when we were discussing the Leyton game. "He was the sort of chap I could have played for."

There were others about whom he was not so generous. Gloucestershire was not always a happy ship in the years after Emmett's retirement in 1958, and I heard occasional rumblings that Arthur was at times among the discontents, even – if the stories are to be believed – the mutineers.

George Emmett was almost 46 years old when he stood down from the captaincy, the last of their pre-war players, a little man who ruled like a martinet, upholding all the traditional values of the game and playing it at all times in an attacking spirit. Arthur was very fond of him, as he was of his predecessor Jack Crapp. "They were our mentors, and they both died quite young. I miss seeing them to talk about those days. I'd just like to see them once or twice a year to revive old memories."

Yet Emmett and Crapp before him were professional cricketers, captaining the county in an era when most other teams still had an amateur in charge. The Gloucestershire committee was not known for its progressive views; it was more a case of lacking a viable alternative.

We will never know what went on in whispered conversations and behind closed doors when George Emmett finally stood down. Later on, he told Arthur that he had recommended him as his successor, but the committee turned to Tom Graveney, another professional and the premier player in the side.

Tom broke a finger halfway through the summer of 1959, and George Emmett returned, with Arthur in charge at Leyton. They finished second in the table, as high as they had been since the days of WG Grace, but they fell away in 1960 when Tom was in sole charge. At the end of the summer the committee took the captaincy away from Tom, and he moved to Worcestershire.

Did the players, Arthur among them, let the committee know that they could do better under another captain, one who had more grasp of how to rotate a bowling attack with three front-line spinners? Or had the committee, even before the appointment of Tom, hatched plans to return the captaincy to an amateur as soon as the opportunity arose? The rumours swirled around the county ground.

Tom Graveney recalls being told that they were going to bring back Charlie Barnett, who was already 50 and had last played in 1948. Mike Eagar, who had played with some success for Oxford University and was now teaching at Eton, was sounded out at some point in the saga. The professionals were given the impression that Arthur was going to be appointed, but in the end the committee opted for an amateur, the 23-year-old Etonian Tom Pugh who had joined the team that summer.

The chronic state of the county's finances was given as part of the explanation to Tom Graveney. There was even a suggestion that Pugh's father, a wealthy businessman, had made, or was going to make, a substantial donation. They were murky waters, and the players gave Pugh a hard time when the summer of 1961 got under way. In mid-May there was a showdown in the dressing room at Lord's, then somehow they started to pull together.

"For the first part of the season Tom Pugh was a complete joke," Arthur said. "But by the end we had got him on our side and trained him. We finished fifth, then fourth the next year. We really warmed to him. He used to talk to us, ask us what we thought. He didn't always do what we said but, whatever he did, it seemed to work. We were a good side. We were playing some really good cricket. Then they slung him out. I was so fed up with that."

Pugh's successor was Tom Graveney's brother Ken, a 38-year-old fast-medium bowler who had not played since 1951, and the downward slide began. After two seasons, in the second of which they finished bottom, they moved on to the quiet John Mortimore, but the side had lost its way by then and the third of his three summers in charge saw them bottom of the pile again. Finally for the summer of 1968 they turned to the man many thought should have had the job all along, Arthur.

It did not work out. He was 40 years old, he struggled with injuries, and the team won only one of the 21 games he captained. David Allen took over at the end of the season but the next year, to the surprise of many, the county turned to Tony Brown. They were not happy times.

"At one stage," Arthur told me, "I wrote to the committee. I said, 'We've had so many problems. The people who know who should be captain are the players. We live in a democratic society. Let the players pick the captain. If they pick the wrong bloke, they're stuck with him so they've still got to do their best. They can change it again the next year.' I've always been a great believer in that, but it's never ever happened."

I have never met a cricketer on the county circuit of those years who did not like Arthur. He was a popular man, a true sportsman who played the game in the best spirit, a kind man with the younger players, one with whom opponents enjoyed a leisurely chat in the bar in the evening, sometimes even a trip to the dog track where he usually tipped winners. It was hard to reconcile all this with the tales of discordance within the Gloucestershire dressing room, the impression that Arthur at times was an awkward character with a lot to say when things went wrong.

"He was always wise after the event," was what Bomber said.

Perhaps the clue lay in what he said to me about his years working as a postman: "It turned me right around, did me the world of good. As a sportsman, playing cricket, you're only interested in your own performance. When you've got to serve the public, it's completely the other way round. They come first. It was an education for me. I learnt from it. It turned me into a better human being."

He was at his best as a batsman when the going was tough, relishing the extra challenge of a batting collapse or an awkward pitch. He was not tall, and he played mostly off the back foot, waiting as late as possible for the ball and guiding it with delicacy into the gaps. 'Arthur Cloth-Bat', they sometimes called him. As late as 1967, when he was 39 years old, he was the leading run-scorer in England, with 2,089 runs and seven centuries. In all, he hit 56 centuries in first-class cricket.

Then there was the close-to-the-wicket fielding. He took 758 catches; only seven people in the history of the game have taken more. "He used to catch shots," Bomber Wells said. "Not just mis-drives and bat-and-pad things. And he'd just toss the ball back to the keeper."

He played till the summer of 1974, more than a quarter of a century on from his first appearance in 1948. In a tribute in *The Cricketer* Alan Gibson called him 'the father of the flock': 'At the age of 46 he still makes his runs and holds his catches.' He showed his younger Gloucestershire team-mates the way with a battling 76 on a lively surface at Worcester, then a patient 51 on a drying pitch at Bristol. His fresh, pink face had lines now; his legs were not as quick as in his Arsenal days. But his batting still had that unruffled composure it had always had and, when conditions were difficult and wickets falling, he still loved the challenge.

His last four innings, in six days in the middle of July, brought only 21 runs: three lbws in the championship and a run-out in the helter-skelter of a Sunday League game at Lydney. His Gloucestershire career had spanned 27 summers. It had taken in 585 first-class matches and 55 one-dayers. And now it was over.

In later years Arthur played more leisurely cricket for Samuel Whitbread's Old England XI, Sunday afternoon games when he took Joan along with him. Tom Cartwright recalled a day when Arthur was summoned at the last minute to make up numbers at Bromyard. "He was in his sixties, and he got his bat out of the attic. He played in his pumps. It was a wet ground, and he never fell over. He had an incredible balance. He got a hundred that day. People like that, days like that, they're very special in your life."

After he retired from cricket he had a spell coaching the Oxford University side. He enjoyed the buzz of being with young, intelligent men, but coaching was not really his forte. "You're born to play," was his view. "Either you can play or you can't play. All the coach can do is recognise that a lad has talent, then encourage him, tell him to watch the good players and to assimilate some of the good things into his own game. Without losing his personality."

Vic Marks was captain of Oxford, and he recalls asking Arthur what he should do if he won the toss. "Well, you could bat, get your runs on the board. Then again you could bowl."

It was much the same when in the late 1980s he helped out the England selectors by watching up-and-coming county players. "Which one would you pick, Arthur?" "Well, they're both good cricketers. ..."

I met his local Conservative councillor. She had tried to canvass him, and he had said firmly that he never voted. "It was good in the war," he told me. "Everybody was all for one, and one for all. There was no party politics."

Everything I ever heard about him fascinated me.

In the summer of 2002 he was awarded an honorary degree by the University of Bristol. By now he was 74 years old, still doing the paper rounds, and the award of this degree moved him greatly. I interviewed him again, this time for an article in *Wisden Cricket Monthly*.

He had just completed a major job on his roof, replacing all the guttering and facia boards. It was the first time he had undertaken such work, and he was glowing with pride at what he had done. It was some minutes before he led me indoors to sit in his conservatory. He was happy enough to talk for a while about his sporting achievements, but it was clear that his real pride that day lay above us around the roof.

His father had worked in a factory in east Bristol, making cardboard boxes, and played cricket for Soundwell, a local team. By the first summer of war Arthur was twelve years old: "The cricket team was always short so I had to take my kit along. Bats were in short supply so Dad cut two or three inches off the bottom of his full-size one. You can imagine how thick that was at the bottom. It turned out wonderful. You could drive the yorker."

At Cotham Grammar his teachers had thought he might win an exhibition to Oxford; another option for him was to be a quantity surveyor. Then an Arsenal scout appeared on the scene, followed by National Service, a contract with Gloucestershire, and for many years he did not give education a thought.

"I've regretted it in my later life quite a lot. But you don't think when you're twenty, do you? You never think you're going to get old. You don't think about things changing. What did Lee Trevino say? 'Unlike golf, you only get to play the course of life once.'"

I guided him on to his Arsenal days. They were the grandest of the English football clubs, the best in the land in everything they did – from the marbled halls of Highbury through to the standards of behaviour on the pitch. They won the championship while he was there, their seventh title, and it took them past the six that Sunderland and Aston Villa had won. He scored nine goals in the campaign, his partnership on the right with Jimmy Logie a vital part of their success.

"It was a hell of a place to be. If you had any ability, they'd get it out of you. They looked after you, too: provided digs, made sure you were OK, wrote to your parents, a great club."

His digs were in Muswell Hill, where he helped the landlady's daughter Joan with her maths homework. She got a job with Barings Bank, and in 1953 they married. He had a lot to thank Arsenal for.

His career at Highbury came to an effective end on a dramatic evening there on Tuesday 9 November 1954 in a friendly match against the Russian side Spartak Moscow. Three years earlier, when he had played against Austria in Wembley, England could boast that no team outside the British Isles had ever beaten them on English soil, but that pride had been shattered in November 1953 when a fluid Hungarian team, led by Ferenc Puskas, had come to Wembley and conquered by six goals to three. Continental football was now seen as ahead of our game, and the visit of Spartak was eagerly anticipated by the Highbury faithful. Sixty-six thousand of them crowded into the stadium that night.

"It was the early days of the floodlights," Arthur said. "They were quite good, except when the ball went above them."

Shortly before half time Jimmy Logie fired home a low shot to give Arsenal the lead, and moments later a cross from Arthur could – should, maybe – have brought a second goal. But the Russians scored twice before the hour was up, and the result pivoted on one never-to-be-forgotten moment. Arthur, at his quick-footed best that night, burst clear into the opposing penalty area and was tumbled over by the Spartak left back. In the spirit of the time the referee was a Russian, and he signalled not a penalty but an indirect free kick for obstruction. The decision, *The Times* reported, 'was greeted by a shrieking whistle, Continental in character and frightening in its intensity, from the vast crowd.'

'It is never pleasant to question such official decision,' the football correspondent wrote, making clear his own view of the incident. 'But in fairness to all, this fact cannot pass unnoticed. It certainly helped to disturb Arsenal, who with greater discipline, might yet have saved themselves.'

He and Logie were in their pomp, stars of the back pages in the popular press, but what followed changed everything. For Arthur, fifty years on, there was contentment on the Downs, delivering newspapers; for Logie, there was none.

"At the end of the game the referee went over to Jimmy to shake his hand, and Jimmy turned away from him. And at Arsenal they really looked down on things like that. He never played for them again. And it ruined his life. He was in love with the club. He finished up selling papers on Piccadilly."

In February Arthur, deprived of his Scottish partner, was transferred to Bristol City, for whom he played fourteen games in an unbeaten run that took them to the championship of the Third Division South. In his last appearance he scored the only goal at Bournemouth. It was his final game as a professional footballer.

"I only played for England because Tom Finney called off. Jimmy Logie broke the news to me. 'Finney's cried off,' he said, 'and they've picked you because you're the nearest to Wembley.'"

It was a nice story, one that suited Arthur's mellow modesty, but it wasn't strictly true. The previous week he had been with an England squad of twenty, training in Manchester. He may only have played twelve times for Arsenal, but they had clearly spotted his talent.

Bomber Wells recalled a Gloucestershire game at Sheffield when Arthur scored a century. Joe Mercer, Arthur's captain at Arsenal and by then the manager of Sheffield United, came into the dressing room, and they asked him, "How good a footballer was Arthur, Joe?" "Oh, he was good all right," was the reply. "He was better than Tom Finney or Stanley Matthews." According to Bomber, he had come in the hope that he could persuade Arthur back into the game.

We talked again about his cricket years. His first two centuries were in 1951 in the two Bank Holiday fixtures against Somerset. In the second of them, in August, Gloucestershire created some excitement by bringing back the great Wally Hammond, 48 years old, suffering from a bad back and five years on from retirement. The crowds swarmed to the Nevil Road ground that Saturday.

Arthur was still in the middle when he came out to bat – "He never said a word to me" – and he watched with sadness as the great man struggled in vain to find his touch. Forgetting himself, the 23-year-old footballer called him for a sharp single, and a photograph survives of the moment, at one end Hammond lunging desperately to complete the run, at the other Arthur turning with a look of horror on his face. "I thought, 'What have I done? I'm going to get lynched.'" Somehow Hammond survived, though not for much longer. "It was terribly sad. I longed to see him do well. But there he was, cursing quietly as he mistimed balls he once hammered."

Such stories, from the heart of our cricketing history, never fail to captivate me. But Arthur, fresh from the ceremony at Bristol University, preferred to talk about that.

"I wish I'd have earned my degree in the normal way and made some use of it. But I was quite flattered. I parked the car, and Joan and I walked down amongst the graduates-to-be, down to the big hall. There were hundreds of them, all having their photographs taken. The Vice-Chancellor came and had lunch with us. It was a privilege to be there, with them all going up to collect their awards. I was the last up. They read an oration, and I had a wonderful response from the hall."

I did not ask him if he had fitted in his paper rounds that morning.

"I deliver the papers to Wills Hall, you know," he said, so tickled by the irony of the degree he now held.

"But tell me, Arthur, if you could go back to being eighteen again?"

"I'd really like to have worked and played. I think that's what sport is for. Recreation and exercise. Away from what you do most of the week. I don't really agree with professionalism."

He had told me before about an MCC Committee, chaired by David Clark of Kent. It had sent out a referendum to all the professionals, asking them what they thought the future structure of county cricket should be. "I said that we should play a three-day game at the weekend, perhaps an occasional one-day game in the week, and we should all get jobs. Firms would have employed you; you could have got somewhere in the working world. A lot of us recommended something like that, but the counties didn't want it so it didn't become public knowledge. One of the troubles with getting anything done in cricket in those days was that it wasn't run by people who played it."

He returned to the subject. "Working and playing, you'd have a different attitude. A lot of the blokes I played with, they were just playing to try to get in the next match, instead of enjoying themselves and putting their own personality on the game. If you have that confidence of 'It doesn't matter', you play better. I was lucky. I had enough talent to be able to do it without any insecurity. I felt privileged to be born with enough talent to take my place in the game I loved. It's not given to many, and it's helped to sustain me in later life. You're not grieving for what might have been."

There was a part of him, however, that was grieving. Not for what he had not achieved on the sporting fields, that no longer mattered to him. But for the time he had spent away from home, the long days at cricket, then the evenings in the bar or at the dog track, the days off on the golf course. He was always out enjoying himself. He had been selfish.

"It's not easy for a wife. It's not a good life for them. I went to Aussie for five months, and David was born while I was away. I was never here when the boys were growing up. That was what was so wonderful about the Post Office. I was home all the time, and we grew closer together. We'd sit down to meals as a proper family. Only the family really matters in life, don't you think?"

How did he come to be a postman? I sensed that a dark shadow had hung over him after he had finished playing. But apart from one brief reference to a road he had looked down and not taken, he never spoke about it.

The coaching at Oxford University was only for a short period of the year, and he had a wife and three boys to support. He helped out a friend, laying floors, but it was only part-time and it never seemed to start till the middle of the day. "I was walking down to Westbury village one morning, and coming up was the postmaster who looked after the sorting office. He was a very good local cricketer, and we got talking. He said, 'There's a part-time job going. You've been outside all your life. It might suit you.' Late '77. It was a hard winter, that year. And it was very steep up and down Falcondale Road. When it was frosty, it was dangerous. I was on my backside more than when I was playing football. Then I took the exam, and they passed me for full time."

He talked in detail about the different rounds, how he came to get the one at Sneyd Park – "the best round in the office" – and how it changed his life. "They were ten wonderful years. It was an education. The education of life."

"Why doesn't Arthur Milton do a book?" people were forever asking me. But nobody could ever persuade him.

There were several writers who would have jumped at the opportunity. Frank Keating would have been superb in his evocatively romantic style. Arthur liked his writing, too. "I only read *The Guardian* for Frank," he told me, "and for the crossword, especially Araucaria. Do you do Araucaria?"

Then there was David Foot, who lived nearby and had been on Arthur's postal round. He was keen, though I suspect he would have wanted to probe Arthur about those lost years between the cricketer and the postman. David Green and Vic Marks, two cricketers who loved Arthur, were both good writers, too.

Why wouldn't he do it? Bomber Wells said it was because he was lazy. David Foot flirted with a theory that he was secretly writing it himself. But his refusal didn't surprise me. It was all of a piece with his delivering newspapers and listening to the old ladies in Cote Paddock.

I was inclined to let the matter lie, but I had a cup of tea at David Foot's house one day and he convinced me that all hope was not lost, that deep down Arthur wanted to do it. "You should write it," he told me. "Give him a ring. I'm sure you could persuade him."

As I drove home to Bath, I composed the opening chapter: Arthur on his bike on the Downs, the narrative flashing back to Wembley and to Lord's, then forward again to the bulky newspapers he was pushing through the letterboxes. A great creative excitement was coursing through my veins.

I rang him with the same sense of intrusiveness that I had had when I found his name in the phone book back in 1997. I felt like a vulture circling unwanted round his life, and I was not surprised when he gave me short shrift. "My memories are my own," he said in that tone of voice he employed when he wanted to close down a line of conversation.

I was asked to chair two meetings of the Gloucestershire Cricket Lovers. The idea was to invite a pair of friends who would talk with each other. We had Ken Taylor and Bryan Stott from Yorkshire, then the following year Roy Booth and Martin Horton from Worcester. Both evenings had a real sparkle, brimming with the warmth of friendship and the special laughter that cricket can generate. On the second occasion Arthur turned up, sitting himself down unobtrusively in the front row.

Roy and Martin were smartly dressed, wearing their Worcestershire ties, but Arthur looked as if he had just come in from a hard day's work in the garden. By the time I got a chance to say hello to him, he was deep in conversation with Martin Horton. "Do you know Araucaria?" he was saying. "He's very good."

The Cricket Lovers asked me to arrange a third such evening, this time with Arthur and Tom Graveney, but that was not so easy. After his sacking as captain Tom had rarely returned to the county's functions, and Arthur inevitably was not keen to stand up and speak. There was much to-ing and fro-ing, and eventually they both agreed a provisional date. Then Arthur suffered a hernia and said he wasn't up to it, Tom became President of MCC, and the idea died a death. I didn't feel like pestering them any further.

One afternoon in late January 2007 the phone rang, and I was surprised to hear Arthur's voice at the other end. Up till then it had always been me ringing him, and we had not spoken for two or three years.

"I've had a couple of health scares, and I've started to see things differently. I've decided I will do a book."

He had asked the Reverend Mike Vockins, who had been secretary of Worcestershire County Cricket Club, to write it. "We've been talking, and we would really like it if you would publish it."

"Of course, Arthur," I said. "It will be a privilege."

Mike kept in touch in the following weeks, complaining that their sessions were not going as he had hoped. Arthur had a booklet that listed the statistics of every first-class cricket match he had played, and he kept reading from that instead of allowing his memory to lead the way.

Then one Tuesday in late April, three months into the project, Mike rang to say they had had a much better session. Arthur had put the booklet down, and the stories had flowed out. Mike, at last, felt confident that he could write a good book.

The following day I drove to Neath. I had just finished a book with Tom Cartwright, and the day before our first promotional event he had had a massive heart attack. It took the ambulance men many minutes to revive him, minutes in which his brain had been deprived of oxygen, and he lay in hospital in a terrible state.

That Wednesday was the sixth of my weekly trips. I had spotted slight improvements each time, but that evening Tom was struggling with a high temperature and slept through most of my visit.

I had a long night ahead of me, having to drive to Leeds, and I stopped for a meal at a motorway service station on the Welsh borders. There I found a message on my mobile phone: 'Ring home. Sue.' When I did, she told me that Arthur had collapsed and died.

Five days later Tom died, too. It was a bad time.

Arthur's funeral was for family and close friends only, but a memorial service followed a few days later. It was held at Westbury-on-Trym Parish Church and was conducted by Mike Vockins. The large church was packed out, and we listened to a tribute by Tom Graveney and to some moving 'reflections' from his son Robert. He told us how he had come to know his father only after the years of cricket were over.

In the autumn of 2009 I published a collection of Alan Gibson's writings, mostly taken from *The Times*, and I was negotiating with the sports desk in the hope that they would carry a feature on the book. "It's difficult," they said. "Space is very tight. We only have fourteen pages for sport."

The next day there were six whole pages on the same football match. Inevitably my mind went back to Arthur and to his England appearance, the single-column report in the ten-page paper.

"Do you realise, Arthur," people would say to him, "if you were young today, with your looks and your sporting talent, you'd be a millionaire?"

He would look at them with a contented smile, perhaps even with a tinge of pity that they had not come to that point of inner peace which he had reached.

"I've been married for fifty years," he would reply. "I've got three great boys, they've all done well, and I've got grandchildren too now. All my life I've had good health, and I was lucky enough to play the games I loved for a living. Out in the sunshine all summer. Then there were the years in the Post Office. Wonderful years, I learned so much from them. Now I'm up on the Downs each morning, watching the sun come up and the mist rising from the dew on the ground. There's nowhere I would rather be."

He would pause for a moment before returning to their question.

"I am a millionaire."

Arthur was Bristol through and through, though he was not blind to the city's faults. "The reps all used to say it was death coming to Bristol. I remember one year the Rovers were having a real good run. We had two papers on a Saturday, the *Evening Post* and the *Evening World*, the pink 'un and the green 'un. One of them printed a letter: 'Why don't Bristol Rovers get more support than they do?" And somebody sent in a reply: 'From what I've seen of the Bristol people, if you give them a free ticket and pay their bus fare, you might get a few of them to go.'"

He chuckled at that, but he said it in the knowledge that he would never move away – certainly not once he had come home from Arsenal, with Joan at his side.

On the wall of his front room there hung a watercolour by the local artist Frank Shipsides. The SS Great Britain coming home to Bristol, the Clifton Suspension Bridge above it.

"When I retired from the Post Office, the residents' association laid on a wine-and-cheese party, and they presented me with this."

I could imagine the scene. He had done much more than deliver their post, I am sure, as he did so much more than deliver newspapers to the ladies of Cote Paddock. Right to the end, though by then I had interviewed scores of former cricketers, he had a way of making me go a little gooey inside, as no one else did. Not because he was the last of the double internationals. No, not that at all. It was the way that he had turned it all around in his later life. He had a lovely way about him; it touched everybody whom he met.

3

GEOFF EDRICH

Will power and a bit of luck

Geoffrey Arthur Edrich

Born: Lingwood, Norfolk, 13 July 1918

Died: Cheltenham, 2 January 2004

It was in many ways the best game in the book and, if I had had my way, it would not have been chosen.

I was travelling around England, interviewing the cricketers of the 1950s, asking each of them to tell me about their most memorable match. By the time I got to Dennis Brookes in Northampton, I was nearing the end of the project.

This would be the eleventh match, and I had now covered all the counties except Northamptonshire and Kent. So I thought to myself, 'Perhaps I can persuade him to choose a match against Kent. Eleven chapters would be perfect.' I had my eye on a 1951 game at Dover, when a ninth wicket partnership of 66 had snatched an unlikely victory for the visitors.

Dennis lived ten doors down from the main entrance to the county ground in Wantage Road, in a redbrick terrace. When I arrived an hour early, he was just about to have lunch. It was a sunny spring day, and I killed time by sitting on the empty terraces at the ground, re-reading Frank Tyson's foreword to the history of Northamptonshire County Cricket Club, with its warm tribute to 'Brookie':

> 'At the end of his career, he was the quintessence of county cricket's senior pro: grey-haired, dignified, accomplished, wise in the ways of first-class cricket and so respected in his local community that he was appointed a JP.'

After a while Dennis appeared at my side, a kindly man in his early eighties, walking with a stick but still sprightly. He spoke with a soft Yorkshire accent, describing the ground as it had been when he arrived for the first time, back in the early 1930s: "Over there was the pavilion, a wooden structure. The secretary's office was at the top. If there'd been a fire, he'd never have got out." He let out a wheezing chuckle. I knew I was in for a good afternoon.

The interior of his house belonged still to the 1950s: the patterned wallpaper in the front room, the ornaments on the mantelpiece, the tea served on a little trolley. I coaxed him towards his choice of match, and he said with some firmness that he wanted to talk about a game at Old Trafford in 1953.

I found it in *Wisden*, and I looked down the Northants team. No Freddie Brown or Jock Livingston, no Keith Andrew, and on the Lancashire side there was no Cyril Washbrook or Winston Place. I was staring at unfamiliar names such as Greasley and Pickering.

For a moment I considered stopping him, trying to draw him away to Dover, but he was already in full flow. The last Test against Australia was about to start. Freddie Brown, the Northants captain, was chairman of the England selectors. The Secretary had warned Dennis the previous day that Brown would declare himself unfit and leave Manchester for The Oval.

"You'd better not include that," he said with another chuckle, but he did not object when I did.

At eight o'clock in the morning the telephone rang in Dennis's hotel room. "I'm sorry, Dennis. I'm not going to play. My wrist has swollen up."

That left them with ten men. A major injury crisis had already depleted the small staff, and they resolved to send for a Peter Pickering who had played an occasional second team game. He was a goalkeeper with Kettering Town and worked for British Timken, whose chairman John Pascoe was the county club's chief benefactor. This match at Old Trafford would be Pickering's only appearance in first-class cricket, and he played well, scoring 22 and 37 in a low-scoring contest.

"The wicket was all scratched to bits," Dennis said. "Lancashire were running for the championship, and they deliberately got a poor wicket. And the trouble in cricket is that the professionals, they see something happening and they think, 'Oh you can't play this shot or that'. Pickering, he went in, he was an amateur cricketer, he just played as if they were schoolboys and he got some valuable runs. He wasn't waiting to see if the ball turned or popped; he just hit it."

It was a lovely story, and it was made all the richer when I tracked down Peter Pickering in Cape Town, from where he sent me a long letter about his life and about the game at Old Trafford. He recalled how in 1940, at the age of 14, he had opened the batting for York with the England cricketer Paul Gibb, and he got to 50 before Gibb had reached 20: 'I was sure then that cricket was to be my life and that one of the three middle order places in the Yorkshire side was mine!!'

As his life panned out, it was football where he made the greater mark. Chelsea paid £7,500 for him, a record fee for a goalkeeper at the time, and he played 27 times for them in the old First Division.

That morning in August 1953 he was in his office at British Timken when the public address system summoned him to see the chairman: 'I arrived there at the double to find his personal secretary waiting for me at the door. She said, "Get in quick, it's urgent." I couldn't imagine what the problem was.'

Home to pick up his kit. A car prepared for him. A long journey to Manchester on the pre-motorway roads. A struggle to persuade the gateman he was playing in the match. A snatched sandwich, and he was ready to take the field in time for the afternoon session. It was a wonderful story. 'The Goalkeeper's Trip to Old Trafford,' I called it. I did think about turning it into a radio play.

Frank Tyson, the raw fast bowler, was in his first summer for Northamptonshire. He had been rejected by Lancashire as injury prone, and this was his first game back there. On the second day, on a bad pitch made even more spiteful by a heavy thunderstorm, he raced in with a wind behind him and bowled flat out. Brian Statham, the Lancashire fast bowler, said he never saw him bowl faster in England.

Northants had achieved a first innings lead of 14, and Lancashire had not cleared the arrears when Tyson took his third wicket. By close of play they were 94 for seven, and the scores of the batsmen dismissed made sorry reading: Ikin 0, Howard 6, Grieves 2, Wharton 4, Marner 5, Hilton 4, Parr 10.

"The ball flew all over the place," Dennis recalled.

I found a passage about the game in Frank Tyson's autobiography:

'It was the closest I have ever come to killing a batsman. Ball after ball lifted from a length to whistle over the batsmen's heads. Very early in the innings I broke Geoffrey Edrich's hand, but he carried on the tradition of his family's guts by batting on.

'This, I thought, was open defiance, and I really let the next one go, pitching it just short of a length. Geoff did not even have to duck. The ball steepled from a length and Brian Reynolds, behind the sticks, rose to it like a trout taking a fly. But the ball refused to be caught and, passing over the tips of his outstretched fingers, it bounced once and hit the boundary boards.'

Peter Pickering's letter added further detail: 'Frank Tyson hit Geoff Edrich countless times on the back of his hand. When he returned to the pavilion and I saw the state of that hand, it looked as though it had been hit repeatedly with a 2 lb hammer. It must surely have been one of the bravest innings ever played.'

At close of play Geoff Edrich was 59 not out. The next morning Bob Clarke, Northants' other fast bowler, knocked the bat out of his hands. Lancashire's final total was 141, of which he contributed an unbeaten 81.

Then Statham set to work with all the speed he could muster, and in a thrilling finish the last Northants pair somehow scrambled the eight runs they needed to win. It was the county's first victory ever in Lancashire, and they stopped the coach on the way home to celebrate with a fish-and-chip meal.

It was Coronation Year. Everest had been climbed, Stanley Matthews had at last won an FA Cup Winners' Medal, and at The Oval Freddie Brown would beam with triumph as England finally won back the Ashes. Meanwhile Peter Pickering returned to British Timken.

Not long after I had written the chapter, an article on Geoff Edrich, by David Foot, appeared in *Wisden Cricket Monthly*. It was in a series called 'Where Are They Now?', and the answer in Geoff's case was Cheltenham, where he had been the cricket professional at the college. In the article Geoff referred to the innings at Old Trafford, saying that Tyson's bowling that day was the fastest he ever faced, so I sent him my chapter, hoping he might offer a few extra comments.

He rang back to say it was all fine. Yes, he remembered the match, and no, he had nothing he wanted to change or to add.

It was a Northamptonshire story, a romantic tale of a club cricketer finding himself summoned to play for his county – in a game Dennis Brookes reckoned to be the very best of the 525 he played. Seen in this perspective, the tale of Geoff Edrich's courageous innings was merely a fascinating sub-plot.

Geoff Edrich lived on the outskirts of Cheltenham, in a terraced house with an old-fashioned cosiness not unlike that of Dennis Brookes's house. I went to see him on the 16th of August 1999.

"Yesterday," he told me, "was the day our war finished. The Jap War. I was in Japan at the end, about 200 miles from where they dropped the bombs. We realised something drastic had happened by the way the Jap guards were behaving. Quite often they were missing."

By this time I had written two books in which cricketers had reminisced about their most memorable matches, one set in the years from 1952 to 1959, the other in the 1960s, and I had an idea to complete a trilogy by going back to the years from 1946 to 1951, those early post-war years of King George VI and the Attlee government.

We sat in his back room, and he selected a Roses match at Bramall Lane, Sheffield. It was the Whit Bank Holiday fixture of 1950, in the summer that Lancashire shared first place with Surrey. It remains their only success in the championship since the war.

"It's not like winning it outright," he said, "but it's some honour. I got a little silver cigarette box with a red rose on it. We had a dinner. You see that photograph there." He pointed to a framed picture sitting on the sideboard. "That was at the dinner."

He had left his native Norfolk almost sixty years before our conversation, but for all his time in Manchester and Cheltenham, the vowels still had a drawn-out East Anglian twang.

"Harry Makepeace was the coach at Old Trafford when I went there in 1946. A double international. He played soccer for Everton and England, cricket for Lancashire and England. He was like a father to the young players, a real good coach, he'd look after the young ones. He always said, if a Lancashire player during his career beat Yorkshire twice, he'd done well. We beat them twice in my career there, but this was my first."

He remembered making runs in the first innings. "I felt in good nick. Then in the second innings I hit one as hard as I could, I really belted it, and I was caught Coxon, alongside the umpire at square leg."

Wisden confirmed his memory.

G.A. Edrich c Coxon b Trueman 70, c Coxon b Close 2

He recalled the great crowd, also the turning point of the match on the last afternoon. Yorkshire were 109 for five, chasing 182 for victory, and their skipper Norman Yardley and the young Brian Close were batting confidently. Then Close called a quick single. The ground was soft and, when he changed his mind in mid-pitch, he slipped and was run out. "Norman Yardley was the last man out," Geoff recalled. "Caught Ikin, bowled little Bob Berry. Apparently, when he got into the dressing room, he said, 'Close, here, I want to look at your boots.' And he didn't have any studs in them."

I had become intrigued by Brian Close, how often he seemed to finish up the main culprit after something had gone wrong, but there was not enough detail in Geoff's memory to create a chapter out of the game.

It was the same with most of the interviews I did for this 1940s book. The cricketers were that little bit older, the time span that much greater, and the formula no longer worked. I settled back on the sofa and let the conversation range over his whole life in cricket.

He talked about his childhood on a Norfolk farm, one of four brothers all of whom played county cricket. "We had a father who loved cricket, and he used to bowl to us. If there was a game of cricket on, the farm would wait."

He talked about his progress into the Norfolk team. He was employed as a professional to coach and to bowl each afternoon to members in the nets at Lakenham. Like his two older brothers Eric and Bill, he made his first hundred against Hertfordshire. And in 1939 he scored a fifty against the touring West Indians: "Martindale was playing. He was a bit quick. Almost as quick as Tyson."

Then came the war. He signed up for the Fifth Norfolks at East Dereham, and he was posted to Liverpool, where he was fire-watching in the docks, at a time when the city was bombed on three successive nights. In 1941 he was sent by boat to the Middle East but, before they got there, the Japanese attacked Malaya and their troopship was re-routed to provide reinforcements there. "We were trained for open warfare so what did they do? They put us in the jungle." He shook his head. "Same as the cricket selectors."

They arrived in January 1942, but they were no match for the Japanese, surrendering on the 15th of February. For a year they were kept in camps in Shangi in Singapore, where life was not too arduous and they played makeshift cricket matches. There were even 'Test' matches, England versus Australia.

In March 1943 they were moved to Thailand, and for two years he worked on the bridge over the river Kwai. "That was the worst time," he said. "Go out at daylight, come back at dusk. Every day. We didn't know what day it was. So many boys had cholera, dysentery, fever. You had to have a bit of luck, same as when you're batting."

He was shipped to Japan, freed by the Americans and came back via Manila, San Francisco and a rail journey across the States. "I got a bit of weight back. It came back quite quickly. November the fifth 1945, we got back to Southampton."

He told the tale with a clipped, matter-of-fact brevity, and I did not press him to elaborate it. I was still looking for a way to write something about his cricket.

His brother Bill had played for England as a 22-year-old in 1938. During the war he had flown a Blenheim, taking part in low-level bombing raids. On the worst sorties one in three did not return. He won a Distinguished Flying Cross, and at the end of the war he returned to Lord's to resume his Middlesex career.

Geoff, however, was 27, his eldest brother Eric 32, and they wondered if they were too late to make it in the first-class game. Eric was a wicket-keeper, who had played occasionally for Northamptonshire in 1945, but the vacancy had been filled, and Hampshire, who had shown pre-war interest in Geoff, were unresponsive. Several further enquiries were unsuccessful, and Lancashire seemed like their last hope.

The county was desperate. The pavilion had been bombed, their appointed captain Jack Iddon had been killed in a car crash, and only four of the 1939 side were still available. The Edriches were given their chance.

"I'd had my first net," Geoff said. "Even before Harry Makepeace had seen me in the middle, he said, 'You're in the thirteen for Slough, Gloucester, Oxford and Cambridge.' That gave me great confidence."

It was a fortnight's tour down south. He was not in the side at Cambridge. Then at Slough, in a two-day match against a Home Counties XI, he was given lbw when he had hit the ball, and he wondered if his chance was gone. But to his surprise he was still in the team at the Wagon Works ground, Gloucester, for the first championship match. He came to the wicket at 73 for three and had scored 21 when Tom Goddard, the tall off-spinner, bowled him a ball that 53 years later he could recall clearly.

"He was a difficult bowler. He didn't give it much air, but he had great fingers and he spun it. I played forward defensive, and I got a very faint tickle onto the pad and up to forward short leg. Charlie Barnett was fielding there, and he caught it. Tom shouted, 'Hooozeeee?" A terrific appeal. The umpire gave me not out, and I stayed. I thought, 'I was given out at Slough,' and I wanted to stay in the side. He bowled another couple of balls which I played, and the umpire called 'Over'. Wally Hammond was at first slip. He used to walk from first slip to first slip like a prince, swinging his arms. He didn't look at me. I wouldn't have minded if he'd looked. He just walked, and I heard this voice, 'Your brother wouldn't have done that.' And I thought,

'This is no good.' I got down the other end, and I waved my bat at one of George Lambert's and the castle went down. I didn't play at it. I wanted to get out. I wanted a tunnel to crawl into. From that day to the day I finished playing cricket I never stayed when I got a touch. If you cheat to win a game of cricket, it's not cricket, is it?"

The question hung in the air.

"What's the good of winning if you cheat?"

I remembered what Tom Cartwright had said about the code of fair play in English cricket in those years: "The war was still so close. People could see the consequences of doing wrong."

It was one of two recurrent themes in our conversation. The other was the importance of being a good team man, helping your mates, encouraging the youngsters.

"In my first Roses match, when I came out to bat, I joined Winston Place, and I was struggling with Arthur Booth, their left-armer. Winston came down to me. 'Look, Geoff, you like the ball coming into you. I can deal with the ball leaving.' He was a very good player of that; I was a bit bottom-handed. 'You keep down Robbo's end, and I'll look after Arthur Booth.' And, through that, we developed a good partnership. He was a great team mate, Winston. If it had been Cyril Washbrook, it would just have been, 'You carry on, sort it out.' If you were batting against Kent, against Doug Wright, Cyril would never be down the end where he had to face him."

Washbrook was the star player in the Lancashire team, but he was a stern disciplinarian. He captained the side from 1954, and it was clear that Geoff had no sympathy for the way he carried out his duties.

"I saved a Roses match at Sheffield in '55. Jack Jordan and I batted out for a draw. Really, Norman Yardley made a mistake there. He bowled Trueman, thinking he could get us. If he'd brought Wardle back earlier, he'd have won the match. After my knock I arrived back to the dressing room, and my first words from the skipper were: 'You're playing for the seconds tomorrow at Keswick.' I'll never forget it. ... Roy Collins was a fine cricketer, but they didn't get the best out of him. They didn't encourage him enough. It's a hard enough game, you want help as a youngster. Give them confidence, make them think they're better players than they are. ... Alan Wharton wasn't a good-looking player, but he was a whole-hearted team man. Cyril didn't give him a lot of credit, but he could bowl for you, just above medium pace, he could field anywhere, and he could bat. He used to hit the ball hard. And he'd give you 100 per cent, which is everything, isn't it? ... We should have won the championship two or three times in the '50s. We had a good enough side, but we never had the leadership."

There was a bitterness in it, just as there was a bitterness that he had never qualified for prisoner-of-war compensation. But my chapter was never written, and his words remained at the back of my mind.

Soon afterwards I wrote a book with Geoffrey Howard, the Secretary at Old Trafford from 1949 to 1964. We looked at the summer of 1956 when Washbrook was recalled to the England side. Geoff Edrich stood in for him, winning six of his ten games in charge, including one in which he astonished everybody by declaring the Lancashire first innings at 166 for no wicket. They went on to win by ten wickets, becoming the first team ever to win a two-innings match without losing a wicket. It was not captaincy in the Washbrook style.

"He always played to win," Geoffrey Howard said. "Cyril played not to lose. Geoff could have been a fine captain. He had a great feeling for the game, and he understood the young players. But there was a time towards the end of each summer when his wartime memories got the better of him."

I heard of an episode at a match at Cheltenham when Geoff was in his seventies. He was talking about motor cars with the umpires, and one of them said how reliable his Mitsubishi was. "They're very clever people, the Japanese." It took the other umpire a few moments to hold Geoff back.

Geoff Edrich played mostly off the back foot, a gutsy player not especially pretty to watch but the best of battlers for his team. He scored 1,000 runs in a season eight times, including 2,067 in 1952.

In 1951 he scored seven centuries, one of them against the touring South Africans whose attack was led by Cuan McCarthy, rated by many as the fastest bowler in the world at that time. McCarthy had a suspicious action that made him even more lethal and, when Geoff had reached 62, he delivered a short ball that reared up and hit the batsman a fearsome blow on the head. But, after retiring for twenty minutes, Geoff returned to take his score to 121.

"He was the batsman to fight hardest of all against the odds," Ken Grieves, his team-mate from Australia, said. "The one man who would never quit no matter how high the odds were stacked against him."

The century was followed by a nine-hour coach journey to Portsmouth where the following morning, his head still throbbing, he was walking to the wicket within half an hour of the start. Later in the day they were clapping another hundred.

It was two three-day games a week. The relentless schedule, after taking them from Manchester to Portsmouth, sent them on to Chesterfield, then to Tunbridge Wells. Then it was back to Manchester for one game before heading off to Colchester and back. Six matches, with each linking journey between 200 and 250 miles. You needed a tough constitution, and Geoff Edrich certainly had that. In nine innings in those weeks he hit four centuries – plus a match-winning 77 at Chesterfield against the awkward pace of Derbyshire's Jackson and Gladwin.

He was also a fine fielder at forward short leg, third in the national catching list the previous summer.

His record in the early 1950s stood comparison with the best batsmen in the country: 1,693 runs at an average of 43.41 in 1951, 2,067 at 41.34 in 1952 and 1,218 at 40.60 in 1953. Only five others – Hutton, May, Simpson, Sheppard and Washbrook – averaged 40 in each of those years.

"As a batsman," he said, "you're at your best in your early thirties."

His summer of 1953 finished early, as a result of his innings against Frank Tyson. At the end of the match he drove to Cheltenham in his Austin 8. The next morning in the dressing room he found he could not grip the bat at all. An x-ray at the nearby hospital confirmed that Tyson had broken his wrist.

'Edrich loves his cricket,' the *Manchester Guardian* wrote of his innings of 81, 'and a man will suffer and risk much for what he loves.'

"You've got to take the rough with the smooth," he told me in his down-to-earth Norfolk drawl. "You have your good days and your bad days. That's all there is to it. It's a character-building game."

His last century came against Sussex at Hove in 1956, the final game of the summer in which he had stood in so successfully as captain. There were twelve of them on the ground before the match, and Washbrook – for whatever reason – planned to omit Geoff from the side.

"If you leave Geoff out," one senior player said, "you'll be left with ten because I won't be playing."

Geoff played, and his hundred in the first innings secured the points that gave them the runners-up position in the championship. At the end of the second day a supporter staged a little cocktail party to celebrate the success, and Cyril Washbrook made an impromptu speech, thanking the key players. At the end of it Malcolm Hilton stood up. "Our skipper's missed one person out," he said. "We'd all like to thank Geoff Edrich." The next morning Washbrook asked him what on earth he meant by chipping in as he did. The fault line in the team was apparent.

I never asked Geoff about that. I found it only recently in a book. But on a lighter note he did tell me how that hundred owed much to the umpiring of his old Lancashire team-mate Eddie Phillipson.

"Eddie was a good team man, one of the ones who'd made me feel at home when I got to Old Trafford. He was umpiring at the bowler's end when

I got to 98. I went to glance the ball. Well, it just flicked my pad, down to fine leg, and the next thing I saw was Eddie signalling a four, took me to 102. The next ball was a real jaffa, bowled me. I said to him afterwards, 'Thanks Eddie.' And he said, 'Well, you might as well have them as leg byes.'"

Geoff was a great believer in the fraternity of cricketers, how they could help each other through life and uphold the best values of the game.

"Freddie Jakeman was umpiring down here at Cheltenham once," he said, recalling the Yorkshire-born batsman who played for some years for Northamptonshire. "We were in the Leckhampton Arms, and he'd had one or two. He was a great man for Rupert Brooke. He was reciting him. 'If I should die, think only this of me.' Very pro-British. And we got to talking about different chaps we'd played with. 'Well, Geoff,' he said. 'Out of every hundred cricketers there's probably two shits. And if the 98 of us can't look after those two, we're a poor bunch.'"

Geoff was a tough man, but he believed with passion in fair play, kindness, team work. To him these were the best of British values.

Geoff was appointed captain of the second eleven in 1957, and he was a great success. 'The youngsters worshipped him,' the journalist John Kay wrote. 'They admired his fighting qualities and his desire to share their joys on and off the field.'

Alas, he stood by them in 1959 when a disturbance in a Birmingham guest house led to a complaint being lodged with the Lancashire committee. A group of them had returned late, a cistern had overflowed, and he was asked to name the culprits. He refused to do so and, despite the pleas of Geoffrey Howard as Secretary, he was out of work. A darkness still haunted him from his war days, and for a while he was desperately low.

He found work at Cheltenham College, as groundsman and coach to the boys, and Geoffrey Howard rang the school. "I said to them, 'Treat him like a master. Don't just use him as a groundsman.' But they didn't take any notice. He wasn't given the status he needed to restore his self-esteem.'

I bumped into Geoff at the Cheltenham Festival while I was writing Geoffrey Howard's book. "They've made me a vice-president at Lancashire," he told me, his pride mingled with a touch of bitterness. "After all this time. And I've had my prisoner-of-war compensation – though not from the right people, not from the Japs."

He was delighted by what Geoffrey said about him in the book and rang to say so.

Lancashire cricket was at its lowest ebb in the 1960s, not reviving till Jack Bond took on the captaincy in 1968 and led them to five one-day titles in four years. Jack was a surprising leader, a quiet Methodist whose contribution with the bat was modest, but he ran a happy team and he always kept up with the position in the game, a vital skill in the emerging one-day format.

"I spent a lot of time with Geoff," he told me. "He was like a father figure to me. A lot of things in my captaincy, I learned from him. Cricket was his life. He'd eat, sleep and drink it. He had such a lot of knowledge. As a captain he was quite prepared to take a gamble. He backed his players on the field and in the committee. Washbrook would let games drift, and that's no good. You've got to get a grip. Cricket is a situations game, and the scoreboard tells you what the situation is. I learnt that from Geoff."

Then Jack spoke about Geoff's darker side, reminding me of what Geoffrey Howard had said.

"People used to drink more in those days. Geoff didn't seem to eat much, and sometimes he'd get upset. It could be something that had happened on the field, often something in the war."

"Christmas 1940, I was at Sandringham," Geoff said. "We were in York Cottage on the estate. The King and Queen were there, and we were on ac-ac duty, with the old bren gun on a tripod. They used to come round with their little corgis and have a chat. Ask us how many rounds we had in the magazine, all that sort of thing. A special unit, pink uniforms. I've got a photograph somewhere."

It was November 2002, and I was once more in his back room.

"I'd wanted to go in the 'raf', but they said, 'We'll put you in the infantry.' So I went to join the Fifth Norfolks in East Dereham."

By late 1941 he was heading on a troopship to the Middle East. The situation in the Far East took a turn for the worse with the bombing of Pearl Harbour, and he found himself in the jungles of Malaya where they were soon forced into a retreat. "We had to come through the jungle back to Singapore Island, but they road-blocked us, you see. We packed in on the fifteenth of February, 1942. It was a bit of a shambles, I'm afraid, the whole set-up. We'd been trained for open warfare."

They were put to work in the docks in Singapore. "You don't do more than you're forced. Later on, up in Thailand, of course, we weren't very fit for work."

Sixty years had passed, years in which the world has moved on, has forgiven and forgotten. We sat on the outskirts of prosperous Cheltenham, and he shared his memories.

"It seems like a bad dream now. It's amazing how we got through it. At a camp called Tarkanon in Thailand we were in old tents on bamboo slats, that's where we slept. I'd had a dose of fever; I hadn't been out to work for a couple of days. I couldn't get up. I looked out, and I saw this boy from the Fifth Norfolks, from Nottingham. He was in our company. This lad was like a skeleton. I was thinking, 'How's he walking?' It was just bones walking. There were only six of my platoon got back. Six out of thirty-odd. I lost twelve in action. Seven of them were knocked out by a bomb from a little plane, five when the Japanese snipers got us. The others died after being taken prisoner. You had to have a bit of luck."

The first year in Singapore was not so hard. They worked six days, then on Sundays they had what the Japanese called a yasume, a rest day when sometimes they played cricket. Their battalion sports officer, Dick Curtis, had carried into the camp a full canvas bag full of cricket kit: stumps, pads, bats and a new ball, and they played matches between the English and the Australians.

He produced a dilapidated scrapbook – "My wife kept it" – and it included an article that said he had scored three successive centuries in those matches. "That was at Serangoon Road, a little camp down in Singapore Town. You just bowled one end. There was no room to bowl from the other. It was like schoolboy playground cricket. It was just something for the boys to watch on the days off."

The scrapbook created a digression, and we left the war to talk about a Commonwealth tour of India in 1953/54. That led him to reminisce about his great friend on that tour, the Gloucestershire batsman George Emmett, another who had had a hard war.

"What a neat player he was. Everything had to be correct. Spot on. Nothing slipshod. I've often been asked the player I'd most like to watch again in full flow, and I always say George Emmett. I've seen Wally Hammond and Don Bradman both score hundreds but, if George Emmett was batting as he can, he was the neatest player of the lot, wasn't he?"

That led him to tell me the story about Hammond at the Wagon Works in 1946. "Your brother Bill would never have done that." He told me how the England batsman Peter Parfitt, in one of his first games for Middlesex, had touched a ball to the keeper and not walked. Geoff's brother Bill was captain, and he told the youngster: "If you do that again, you're not in my team."

That was the spirit of the game in those years, and he was sad that it was no longer so. "I don't know what the reason is. Whether it's money. Whether it's the love of the game. Do they think as much of the game as we thought of it?" The sing-song rhythm of his Norfolk vowels gave the question an extra poignancy.

I could offer him no answer so, after a pause, I returned to 1946.

"It says here that you spent that first summer on a 20% disability pension."

His reply was slow and slightly faltering.

"Yes, I think I did. … Olga had been on a widow's pension during the war. … I'd been dead for a couple of years. … There you are. That's life, isn't it? … What is to be is to be. … You have to have a bit of luck to get through – and a bit of will power, I suppose. … Anybody can lay down and die. … A lot of the boys died of a broken heart, actually. They couldn't see the end. If you thought, 'This is not going to finish,' that's it, isn't it?"

"And you kept going?"

"Well, yes, with the help of one or two pals. One of my pals, he's still alive, I think. Dick Stewart from Fakenham. One march up from Tarkanon to another camp called Tarso, it's about 20 or 30 kilos. We had to march, and it was tipping down. One or two were ready to pack in, but he said, 'Keep going.' If you dropped out, that was it. You got a bloody bayonet through you from the Japanese guards. With his help I eventually got there. But I don't think I'd have got there without his help. Probably I helped him once or twice. You had to have a lot of luck – and one or two decent chaps with you. That's probably what made me always feel that to have success at cricket, you've got to have team spirit, haven't you? And all the players have got to like the skipper and respect him. They won't play for you if they don't."

We were entering familiar territory.

"I shouldn't say this, but I will. That's why under Washbrook Lancashire didn't win anything. He played cricket as they used to do before the war."

"What did he do in the war?"

"Oh, I don't know. He was a PT instructor or something."

"You must have felt, coming back, that some people had had easier wars."

"That's the luck of the draw, isn't it? You can't plan your life. You just take what comes."

We returned to the cricket in Singapore. After Serangoon Road came Changi on the Penang, where the cricket was of a higher standard. There was a complete ground with a worn matting strip, and they played an Australian side captained by the Test cricketer Ben Barnett. England won 2-1, and Geoff scored 65 in one of the matches. Jim Swanton turned up while they were playing, he saw Geoff run up to bowl with his rushing, slingy action and he thought it was brother Bill.

I read to him what he had said in the article: "We were prisoners no longer. It was a Test match between England and Australia, and that was it. All of us forgot everything else."

Dick Curtis the sports officer even had access to a typewriter, and the team sheets were beautifully printed. It was serious cricket, but it all ended in early 1943 when they were taken up the line to Thailand, to the building of the bridge. For eighteen months Geoff laboured there.

"Time goes on, doesn't it? Work, sleep, bit of rice, work. It's amazing what you can put up with, really. A lot of them didn't, mind. You have to have somebody looking after you. There was fever, dysentery, cholera. Tropical ulcers were a bad thing, too. When you were cutting the jungle down for the rails, if you got a bamboo scratch, it used to form these ulcers. There must be some poison in the bamboo. They used to grow quickly from a shilling to half a crown. There was no anti-sceptic. They used to lose their limbs. There was one place where …"

His voice trailed away.

"Oh dear, it was terrible. But it's one of those things. War is war, isn't it?"

In August 1944 they were taken to Japan, to work in the shipyards there. "There were eight or nine ships in our convoy, and only three of them got through to Japan. We were shipwrecked off Formosa. We ran aground. Another ship came along, and we were roped from one ship to another. Another bit of luck."

Eventually the war was over, and he returned to England – but not immediately to Olga and their boy Barry.

"I went home to my parents in Buckinghamshire. My father was managing a farm down there. I played my first season at Old Trafford, then Olga and I got together again. It was a complete upheaval. Olga had been assuming I'd been dead."

He regained his strength with good farm food and pints of Guinness, then started his new life at Old Trafford.

"I didn't talk about the war for a number of years. I tried to put it out of my mind completely. You lost so many pals. It's best left, isn't it? … Now? Well, now my memory is starting to go."

He told me he had had cancer of the throat. For eight years he had not eaten a solid.

At the end of my visit we returned to the match against Northamptonshire.

"If I was asked the best innings I played in my career, that would be the one. There was rain on a hard wicket, and it was a flyer. Tyson was Lancashire born, and we'd let him go. When he'd played for the seconds, he'd had a bit of back trouble. They sent him to a specialist in Manchester, and he said, 'This man will never play six days a week.' Something silly like that. So when he gets back to Old Trafford and he gets us on this wicket, he thinks, 'I'll show this Lancashire lot.'"

Once more I read the other scores: Ikin 0, Howard 6, Grieves 2, Wharton 4, Marner 5, Hilton 4, Parr 10.

"At Old Trafford, when you watch from the pavilion, it's side on and it looks far worse than it is. The players coming in to bat were seeing these balls fly all over the bloody place, and they didn't fancy it. They didn't want to know really."

Statham was the next man in.

"I said to Brian, 'You're not coming to this end. You're not coming to Tyson. I'll take Tyson, and you can take Bob Clarke.' And about second ball Clarky knocked his bloody cap off. He said, 'I'll be better down that end, Geoff.' I said, 'You keep down there, mate.' Tyson was a bit frightening, but I played a lot in that innings by instinct, really. You had to watch it go past your ears but, if it came, if you played with a loose bottom hand, if you got a touch it went to ground. It was the only way of surviving."

I repeated Peter Pickering's description of his wrist looking like it had been hit repeatedly by a two-pound hammer. "No, no, that's all wrong," he said. "I drove down to Cheltenham. I couldn't have done that if it had been that bad. I didn't even realise it was broken. But I couldn't grip the bat for a long time afterwards. In fact, I couldn't grip correctly till I got to India that winter."

We sat in silence for a little while.

"There we are," he said. "It all comes down to how much you want to play."

"Like when you were a prisoner of war. You said that was all about wanting to keep going."

"Plus the fact you've got to have a bit of luck."

The words echoed round my head. "It's amazing what you can put up with, really. … You've got to have team spirit, haven't you? … Decent chaps with you. … Will power to get through, and a bit of luck. … Anybody can lay down and die. … It all depends how much you want to play. … Do they think as much of the game as we used to do?"

In his scrapbook I found the newspaper article by Ken Grieves, the one which described Geoff as 'the batsman to fight hardest of all against the odds, the one man who would never quit.' It was a glowing tribute, the more special for being written by a team-mate.

Geoff Edrich might not have been an elegant batsman, not somebody whom spectators would queue up to see, but in the eyes of his fellow cricketers he was a bloke you wanted on your side. Ken Grieves called him 'the ideal club man' and 'an excellent skipper'.

"I'm very proud of that article," Geoff said.

Wells, bowled Titmus
Lord's, 1954
The keeper is Leslie Compton

4

BOMBER WELLS

The exaggeration and the gist

Bryan Douglas Wells

Born: Gloucester, 27 July 1930

Died: Gloucester, 19 June 2008

Bomber was a large man, and he sat in a large armchair in prime position in the front room of his 1960s house.

"Take a pew," he said to me in his broad 'Glorster' voice. His wife Mary went in to the kitchen to make me a cup of coffee.

An old, black cross-collie dog lay on the rug at Bomber's feet, and I made myself comfortable on the sofa. I was sitting at a ninety-degree angle to Bomber who occasionally looked across to me but mostly, while he was speaking, he stared out of the front window across to the Gloucester ring road in the distance.

"Have a custard cream," he said, helping himself to several. "What do you want? Stories?" And he was away.

I had been working on my book for two months, and I was still rather nervous when I rang up cricketers. "I won't stay more than two hours," I would say apologetically. I would record the conversations on a little cassette recorder, bringing with me two 90-minute tapes. That morning, however, for some reason I brought a third tape. I had a funny feeling it was going to be that sort of session.

Bomber began with the story of his debut match at Bristol in 1951, a story I had already heard in part from Arthur Milton.

"I was courting, and I was out in the park in Gloucester. And we were having some fish and chips. It was a lovely evening. We were sitting on a bench, about half past nine or ten o'clock, and this huge chap came across. I thought, 'I recognise him.' It was Tom Goddard; his picture was in the paper every other day. He came up to me and he said, 'Are you Bomber Wells? Get down to Bristol tomorrow. You're playing against Sussex.'"

This led to a digression on the different levels of cricket: club, county and Test. "It was just like I was playing for Gloucester City against Bath or Stroud. You don't know what they can do so you go out to show them what you can do. … Nowadays, if you play county cricket, you've got to be trained to play Test cricket. But there's no difference. It's just another day, that's all."

Mary got up and fastened a lead round the neck of the collie dog. "Come on, Midge," she said. "Let's go for a walk."

Bomber, in the meantime, had got onto the subject of Arthur Milton's football. "He never got a pass in his England game. That's sad, isn't it?"

Then it was George Emmett: "The greatest captain I've ever known in my life. He read the game. He was a hunter, he went out for the kill. He'd prefer to lose the game trying to win it than not have a go at all. He was marvellous – but he was a real disciplinarian."

That led to a story about a match at Hove, when after heavy rain the captains had agreed to move the pitch to the edge of the square. "Cooky and

I were going down to Brighton for the day. Old Emmett said, 'Where are you two going? We're playing.' He never gave up, and Marlar the Sussex skipper was mad as a hatter. A superb bowler, mind you. If he'd have played for us or Glamorgan, instead of on those little green 'uns at Hove, he'd have taken 130 or 140 wickets a season."

Bomber was like a great Catherine wheel, going round and round, sending off sparks and flashes in every direction. His stories all made liberal use of exaggeration, but beneath that there was an earthy humour and a sharp eye on the human race.

"We declared and left them an impossible target. The pitch was turning and lifting, and the idea was for Cooky and me to rub the ball in the dirt, which you could do in those days, and get stuck in. But we were right on the edge of the square: about 27 yards on one side, 150 the other way. And they had Don Smith, a left-hander who was a real on-side Harry."

The story went on. Derek Hawkins, a part-time off-spinner, had a couple of overs, and Smith hit him several times over the short boundary into the crowd of members sitting in front of the pavilion. By this stage I had found the page in *Wisden*, and I saw the figures: Hawkins, 2 overs for 33 runs.

"You've never seen such an exodus from the pavilion. 'Well tried, Derek,' Emmett says. 'Take a rest.' And he brought me back. And Smithy hit this six. A skimmer. There was hardly anybody left in the pavilion, but it hit this chap straight in the mouth, and they all started rushing round, loading him up on a stretcher. Then this other chap runs onto the field with a little umbrella. 'That man there,' he says, pointing to me, 'will get someone killed. You've got to take him off. I'm insisting. He's a danger.' He even tried to hit somebody over the head with the umbrella. In the end Marlar hauled him off. Then Smithy hit another six, the stretcher bearer ducked and the poor chap in the stretcher fell out. They were amazing scenes."

With Bomber as narrator, the world of 1950s county cricket was never short of incident or character.

"The umpires then, they umpired for the love of the game. If people deliberately padded up, they would give them out, irrespective of whether it was going to hit the wicket. After the game they'd say, 'Look, son, you've got a bat in your hand, that's what the bugger's for.'

"The funniest was Alec Skelding. He was the first one to wear white boots. And he always had a hip flask. We were playing at Leicester. It was a pig sty in those days; fielders in the outfield usually wore a box. And it was absolutely bitter. An evil wind was coming over the pavilion, down the ground, and it wasn't raining hard enough to go off. Everyone except the players was inside. And the ball was wet through. 'Hold it,' Alec said eventually. 'Hold it.' He walked up to the pavilion. Not a soul in sight, just this one white-coated gateman, sat by this gate. 'Excuse me,' he said. 'Do you mind closing that door, 'cos there's a hell of a bloody draft coming out.'"

Mary returned with the dog and went into the kitchen. Then after a while she reappeared in the front room. "How are you getting on?"

"Ooooh, grand," Bomber said, and he was off with a story about a game against the mighty Surrey at the Wagon Works ground in Gloucester when Harry Baldwin, who had played briefly for Surrey in the 1920s, was umpiring. "He hated Surrey. They'd done him wrong. If you listened to him, he always reckoned he was a better player than Jack Hobbs. He really resented the way they'd treated him. Cooky was bowling at his end. And Harry came over to me. 'Your mate never appeals for anything, does he?' I said, 'He does if he thinks they're out.' He said, 'Oh, bloody appeal. *They* all do.'

"I had a word with Cooky. He was bowling at Bernie Constable. Bernie used to come outside the line of the ball and, if he missed, it would bounce away off his pads. And this ball hit him. He must have been five yards down the pitch and, as he was turning back to his crease, Cooky said, 'How's that?' And Harry said, 'Bernie, you're out.' You should have seen the look Bernie gave him."

It was the sort of thing I had come across occasionally in club cricket, but it was hard to believe that it went on in the first-class game. Yet, when I met Bernie Constable a few weeks later, in a pub near Sandown Park, he knew straightaway what I was talking about.

"Harry Baldwin? He done me several times. I upset him once, and he done me the next game. I'm sure he did. Illingworth of all people, bowling round the wicket. He hardly turned the ball at all, Illingworth. … He was a bumptious little man. He had a trilby hat. I'm certain he took a dislike to me."

"After the game," Bomber continued, "their skipper Stuart Surridge came into our dressing room. He was having a drink, and old George Emmett said, 'I'm sorry about that.' And Stuart says, 'Don't worry. He does us three times every year. We know we're going to get done with him.'"

"I'll take Midge out again," Mary said and left us to it.

Next came a second eleven game against Bristol University. "A two-day so-called friendly," Bomber called it. "It was like Hitler versus the Jews, that sort of atmosphere. They had this red-headed chap batting, and he started arguing with Bobby Etheridge, our keeper. Over after over. 'I want a word with you,' he said at the end, and Eth said, 'Bugger off'" and hit him with his wicket-keeping glove. And this chap, it turned out he was wearing a wig. This great mop of red hair went flying off, and they started chasing each other all the way round the university ground. And who should turn up while all this was going on but Old Emmett? He'd come to see how we were getting on."

Bomber's stories piled incident upon incident; he never seemed to pause for breath. There was a story about a boundary catch he had taken with one hand while drinking a cup of tea, a story about Wilf Wooller at Cheltenham barracked by the crowd and sitting down on the pitch, and a drinking contest at the County Hotel, Taunton, when 'Cooky' had been sick and they had had to fish his false teeth out of the toilet bowl.

Mary returned with the dog.

"Do you want a spot of lunch, Stephen?" Bomber asked, and he continued as he munched his way through some cheese-and-tomato rolls.

"They were lovely days. Youngsters today, they can't envisage it, can they? You could bat and bowl as you liked. There wasn't the coaching so people had to work out their own ways of scoring. Everybody had their own bread-and-butter shots. It's another world now. Everything's got to be done according to the book."

I had arrived at ten o'clock, and by a quarter to three the final tape had run out. So I took to scribbling as much as I could on bits of paper.

"We weren't light-hearted. Far from it. No one ever gave you anything. It was played harder then than it is now. But you appreciated each other's skills."

The stories had a roughness about them, as befitted a boy from the back streets of Gloucester, but deep down he was in love with the romance of cricket, especially the slower game that they had played back in the 1950s. He loved the manners of it all – and the aesthetics.

"When I played, it was a much gentler society. People had time. They'd sit and watch the game and appreciate it. Now, with these Sunday matches, it's like a football crowd, isn't it? I remember speaking at a dinner for Neville Cardus. The limited-over game had been going for two or three years. Millions of words had been written by every Tom, Dick and Harry, trying to describe it. And I said to him, 'Right then, Neville, what do you think of the limited-over game?' He thought for a few seconds, then he said, 'It's like trying to play Beethoven on a banjo.' I thought, 'Great. He's summed it up in just a few words.' These great people can do that, can't they? It makes you feel very humble when you're in front of greatness, doesn't it?"

I was due in Stroud at four, for a net with Ken Biddulph, so at half past three I stood up. "I'm afraid I've got to go now, Bomber."

He looked quite shocked. "But I haven't finished telling you the story of my debut match," he said with a touch of aggression.

So I sat down again, and he carried on. The dog went for a third walk, we had tea and biscuits, and I got away some time after five.

Bryan 'Bomber' Wells played for Gloucestershire from 1951 to 1959, then for Nottinghamshire from 1960 to 1965. He is known now as one of the funniest men ever to play cricket, perhaps the funniest of them all, both for his antics during his playing days and for his story-telling in the years after. As a result people tend to overlook that he was actually a very fine off-spinner.

He took 122 wickets in 1955, 123 in 1956. For several years he kept the future England cricketer David Allen out of the Gloucestershire side. Then, when Allen finally replaced him in 1959, Bomber moved to Nottingham, the least bowler-friendly track in the country. Without the help of Bristol's sandy pitches, many feared for him, but in his first summer at Trent Bridge he took 120 wickets. Among off-spinners, only Don Shepherd of Glamorgan captured more. Reg Simpson, the Notts captain, called him 'the most complete off-spinner in the country', advocating his selection for the Test team: 'If we wanted a genuine England side with character,' he wrote in his column in the *Nottingham Evening Post*, 'Wells would be in my side every time.'

He was overweight, short-sighted and inclined to play the fool. His Labour politics were not to the taste of many, either. As a fielder he was lumbering; as a batsman, rustic. Even as a bowler he did not look the part, approaching the crease off a shuffling run-up that consisted of barely two paces. He turned back to his mark and returned in a little circle which, in the words of Jim Swanton, had 'half the circumference of a portly umpire'.

Yet he had a perfect action at point of delivery, and with his strong shoulders he could send the ball down much faster than the batsmen anticipated. He had big hands, and he could bowl a whole variety of deliveries: not just off-breaks but floaters, seamers, leg-breaks and all. He also had a sharp cricketing brain; he loved the battle of wits between bowler and batsman.

It was his misfortune to play for Gloucestershire in the same years as David Allen and John Mortimore, both of whom went on to play for England. Yet I have met quite a few cricketers of that time who have told me that, as a bowler, Bomber was the most dangerous of the three.

The story of his debut match has become the stuff of legend, repeated and elaborated by all and sundry in after-dinner speeches up and down the country. He came down to Bristol on the bus, with his kit in a brown paper bag, and he strolled into a dressing room where almost no-one had ever set eyes on him before.

The captain was Sir Derrick Bailey, a wealthy Herefordshire farmer whose father had owned diamond mines in South Africa, and he went through all his options before giving Bomber a chance: Lambert and Scott with the new ball, Mortimore for off-spin, a few overs of seam-up from Arthur Milton, even a little three-over spell himself. Then after lunch he threw the ball to Bomber.

Such was the speed with which Bomber got through his deliveries that they say Sir Derrick walked in from mid-off for the first ball, turned, went back to his mark and walked in again … for the third ball.

Sussex had taken lunch at 120 for one, but the wickets were soon falling. David Sheppard, lbw to one that scuttled on; George Cox, bewildered by a prodigious leg-break. The Sussex batsmen had not seen his like before, and by early evening Bomber was leading his team off with six wickets to his name.

In all he bowled 61 overs in the match. At the end, they say, he made a little speech in the dressing room. "Well, I can see I'm going to be doing a lot of bowling if I play for this team. I shall have to cut down my run-up."

A Surrey batsman of the early 1960s described beautifully the sight of Bomber bowling: "What a character! He looked like Bud Abbott. The lower he went to the ground, the wider he became. And what a bowler! He didn't half spin it, and he was fairly brisk. If he hit you on the leg, he hurt you. He just stood at the wicket and turned his arm over. John Edrich had this ritual. He always looked down three or four times when the bowler was in his run-up. Well, Bomber would be standing there, ready to let the ball go. I can see him now. 'Are you ready, our John?' he'd ask in that broad Gloucester accent, and John couldn't get his four nods in. They just couldn't get in synch."

Arthur Milton had a story about a game at Bristol against Leicestershire:

"Bomber's bowling from the pavilion end at this left-hander Goodwin. And Goodwin hits this ball out to deep mid-off. They go for a second run, and there's a run out on at Bomber's end – but, instead of standing behind the wicket, he's stood in front. The bloke's only halfway down when the ball comes in, but it hits Bomber on the shin and runs away. And Bomber's bouncing around for about five minutes. 'Well, skip,' he says eventually, 'I can finish the over but I won't be able to run up.' Well, that was funny enough. But then he puts one foot on either side of the wicket, brings his arm over, bowls him out and off we go. He really was a phenomenon."

Bomber had a wonderful story about a game at Worcester when he contrived with Roly Jenkins, another cricketer who never stopped talking, to get through a full over while the cathedral clock was striking twelve.

"What do you think you're doing?" Sir Derrick Bailey asked him.

"Not a lot."

"You're making this game look stupid."

"I'm not. That's what I normally do."

"I want you to go back ten yards. Come in from further back."

"I thought to myself, 'I can do better than that.' I can bowl it from there. Because that's what he actually said. 'Come in from further back.' So I went back ten yards. I stood still, and I bowled it from there. You've never heard such laughter at a cricket ground. George Emmett at short leg, he was doubled up. But Sir Derrick went berserk. He dropped me for two matches afterwards."

Bomber's priorities were clear: "It was worth it, though."

I was never sure how much of it was true. But then I would meet up with another cricketer, one who was not prone to such exaggeration, and he would tell a Bomber story every bit as ridiculous.

David Allen had one about a game at Bristol when George Emmett was the skipper. The pitch was taking turn, so he rubbed the new ball on the ground and asked Bomber to take the first over from the orphanage end.

"Emmett crouched down at short leg, looking at the batsman, and the batsman didn't seem to settle. So he said, 'Are you not ready?' 'I'm ready all right,' he said. 'It's your bowler who's not ready.' Emmett turned round, and there was Bomber, walking right back to the boundary."

"What are you doing, Bomber?"

"I've got the new ball, haven't I?" came the reply. "I've got to run in."

"Can you imagine? Bomber running in from the boundary. It wasn't just one ball, either. The whole pantomime went on for about an over and a half."

Bomber loved my book, with its collection of amusing stories, its fondness for the lost golden age of his youth. He even contributed a little quote for a promotional leaflet I was preparing: 'My wife will definitely buy a copy.'

At our first meeting he had told me about a novel he was writing, a sort of cricketing version of Dick Francis's horse-racing thrillers, set in the 1950s in the world of county cricket. There were two main characters, he explained: the hero and the 'baddie'. The baddie loses part of a leg in a car accident, becomes bitter and twisted and devises a scheme to sabotage the career of the hero.

"The book takes you through a season in those days. But it's the tenses that catch you out, isn't it? My mind will dash back forty years, then Mary who's doing the typing, she'll suddenly say, 'Hold on, that's the wrong tense. 'Is' should be 'was', 'you' should be 'he'."

I had not been able to find a publisher for my book so I had done it myself. And that immediately gave Bomber an idea. Perhaps I could publish his novel.

Three days before Christmas 1997 I met him and Mary at Easton-in-Gordano service station on the M5. They handed me a supermarket carrier bag with about 800 typed pages in it.

"How many words is it?" I asked, rather taken aback.

"About 200,000," Mary said. I got the impression that she had typed and retyped it several times.

It was an extraordinary work. In some passages it used the real names and places of cricket: Compton and Shackleton, Lord's and the Wagon Works. Then it would spiral off into the most fantastic plot, with the main character undergoing a complete change of identity. It would have cost a fortune to print, and I really had no confidence that it would be the best seller he imagined.

I rang him some weeks later with my verdict.

"Why don't you do a book of stories about your own playing days?"

"Right, we'll do that then," he said.

So I was doing that.

He started with his childhood in New Street, Gloucester, the games of cricket they played during those wartime evenings of Double British Summer Time.

"To me, when I was young, it was a big street. You look at it now, and everyone's got a car. And you wonder how the hell you ever had room to play cricket. It looks so narrow, it's incredible. And the doors are all shut and the windows closed. In our day people used to sit outside on the chairs. The women would sit there, drinking their cups of tea. And nattering. The same conversation would start at one end and go all the way down to the other."

We had two sessions in March 1998, and they were as magical as any two sessions I have ever had as a writer. He could talk on and on, almost without pause, one thing leading to another, and he had none of that veneer of middle-aged respectability or acquired language that would have distanced the world he was describing. Somehow, sitting in that armchair, he was happy to be once more that boy in New Street.

"I can see them now, my dad and his brothers. Sitting around the coal fire. Our dad sat there in his grandfather chair, flanked by my uncles. And there I was on the lino floor, listening."

Bomber had never had children himself, and he managed to be both the child he had once been and his father holding forth from the grandfather chair.

"I listened to them talking about Charlie Parker, Wally Hammond, Tom Goddard, all those great Gloucestershire cricketers. My uncles would come round in the winter, and I would sit by the fire and visualise these great gods. Charlie Parker: if he couldn't bowl them out with his spinners, he could bowl them out with his seam. Wally Hammond, so brilliant he could play the ball with just the edge of his bat. Tom Goddard, he could spin it from one side of the pitch to the other."

I was transported as he talked: sitting on that lino floor, listening to his every word.

"They'd have a crate of beer on the table, a couple of dozen bottles, and they'd down the lot. And all the time they'd be talking about cricket. Picking their best England team, that sort of thing. And the more they had to drink, the more Gloucestershire players there'd be in the side. And I just listened. I never realised it, the actual effect it was having on me at the time. When you're young, you don't realise you're taking it in, do you? You don't realise what you're storing away in your cranium."

He recaptured the past with brilliant vividness but, whenever I settled into a comfortable nostalgia, he would flash out a comment about present-day life.

"If we got hold of a bat, we'd drop it handle first onto the pavement, see how many times it bounced. Boom-boom, that's a two-springer. Boom-boom-boom, that's a three-springer. 'That's a better bat, that's a three-springer.' They were all things that kids did in those days. You lived in a world free of all this intense commercialism. You lived in your little world, and you were satisfied with your lot."

The sessions started off on a specific topic, but soon they were all over the place.

"I could bowl standing still. If you're a natural, everything comes easy. You can do what you like and get away with murder. If you're coached, unless you stay in that groove, you're struggling, aren't you?

"People put Hammond on a pedestal. 'Oh he won't speak to us.' And it's stupid, isn't it? Compo and Sobers, they'd mix with anyone. In the end, Wally only brushed shoulders with lords and ladies, aristocracy. If only from the start it had been, 'Ah, Wally'. People can be cruel like that."

There was a great life-force running through everything he said. He was a free spirit, letting himself go, and I loved listening to him.

Our next meeting came on the first evening of Ken Biddulph's annual coaching weekend in the Cotswolds. He had asked Bomber and me to say a few words after the meal.

At the table I sat next to Bomber, who talked away with gusto while we ate. Ken was at the other end. He loved Bomber, but he was on edge that evening. His fellow coach had let him down, and he was more than usually concerned that everything should go smoothly.

Bomber was a strict teetotaller, but he did not need alcohol to get him going and, as the meal progressed, he got into a line of stories that all had something of an anti-establishment flavour to them. The chap across the table from me, a lad from Derbyshire, was clearly enchanted. "Tell me," he said. "Why has Fred Trueman never got a knighthood? Is it because he's too left wing?"

"Left wing," Bomber repeated at full volume. A couple of peas shot out of his mouth across the table. "Fred? Left wing?" By this point the whole table was listening to him. "He's a bloody fascist."

I glanced towards Ken, whose face was a picture of panic. "I think it's time to hear Stephen speak," he said hurriedly.

Once I had given my short talk, the conversation at the table was calmer. Bomber talked about promising young players, and I asked him how he could tell whether somebody had real talent.

He hesitated before replying. Then he came up with one of those lovely, off-the-wall lines that only he could dream up.

"You get a tingling feeling in the nape of your neck."

Soon afterwards he and Mary came down to Bath for a meal with us, and I told him that I was going to be busy for a couple of months. "I'm going to leave things till later in the summer. Then I'll get down to the book in earnest."

In June Mary rang. Bomber had had a bad stroke. He was in the Gloucestershire Royal Hospital, and he would not be out for quite some time.

"I'll understand, Stephen, if you don't want to go on."

Bomber was a tough character, and he made a better recovery than anybody had thought possible. He was in a wheelchair, and his speech was slower. But we resumed work the following year, and I got into the habit of going up to his house every Tuesday morning.

The sessions became more and more rambling; I became less and less clear how to turn it all into something. We just kept meeting. I started to hear stories for the second and third times, but there was always something new each visit. So I convinced myself we were making progress.

It was February of the following year, after eight months of this, when he suddenly stopped in mid-story. "Are we doing a book, or what?"

It gave me the jolt I needed. I came up with the idea that the book would be set at Cheltenham in 1999, with Bomber on the boundary telling the story of a 1957 match there. It would read as if we were sitting among the spectators, talking away as one does at cricket, with each interval in play providing a self-contained digression. I worked in other voices – Tom Graveney, Arthur Milton, George Emmett's daughter, a Cotswold forester and more – as if they had joined us on the boundary.

"What a lovely, simple way to write a book," one reader said, thinking that it had happened just like that; I had simply turned up with a tape recorder and typed out the conversation. I did not have the heart to tell him of all the hours I had spent in Bomber's front room, wondering how on earth I would ever make any shape of it all.

We held the launch in a marquee at Cheltenham. George Emmett's sister and daughter came up from the West Country, and Bomber parked his wheelchair next to the sister, Joyce. "Now then," he said with a twinkle. "Are you the sister or the daughter?" It was the perfect start, and it got better. "There's never a day goes by at Cheltenham when you can't walk round the ground and hear somebody talking about some innings by your brother."

About that time the county gave a benefit to their long-serving groundsman at Bristol, David Bridle. A brochure was produced, with contributions from many distinguished players, all on the theme of favourite cricket grounds. They wrote about Lord's and Melbourne, Cape Town and Barbados. Bomber was the only one who chose to write about Bristol.

At the launch he made a special fuss of the 87-year-old forester, Charles Light, whose memories of the Cotswolds and of the Cheltenham Festival in the 1920s added a whole dimension to our book. Charles had grown up in a feudal world, long before the Agricultural Workers' Wages Act of 1947, and for all his intelligence he was overawed by the company in the marquee. In the eyes of Bomber, though, he was the most important person there.

Bomber had persuaded me that we should price the book at eight pounds. He did not think people would be able to afford ten. Then at Cheltenham he sat in his wheelchair and, each time he sold a copy, he seemed to be offered a ten-pound note. "People have got more money than I thought," he said.

"I'll tell you what," he would say, reaching into his top pocket. "I won't give you change. I'll give you two pounds worth of these raffle tickets for Gloucester City Cricket Club." I bought some every time we met that summer, and I finished up winning two prizes – though one of them, two bottles of beer, he managed to smash on his front path.

"I wasn't even going to buy a copy," a woman complained to me. "And he was sitting there, telling me he'd written me a dedication." For all that, she finished up seeing the funny side of it. It was hard not to with Bomber.

We had a glowing review in the *Daily Telegraph* from Michael Parkinson: 'Bomber Wells,' he wrote. 'There was a summer's day in his face and laughter in his soul.' When I read it, I felt just as Bomber had done all those years before with Neville Cardus. 'Great. He's summed it up in just a few words.'

I had made a repeating feature in the book of the way he kept pressing food onto me. "Have an apple, Stephen ... No, thank you, Bomber ... Go on, take it." So I was most amused when I went for the six-monthly check-up on my teeth to discover that my dentist had bought the book and that this exchange about the apple had caught his imagination.

"We're saying it to each other all the time at home now."

There was a filling to be done, and my mouth became cluttered with a suction tube and cotton wool around the gums.

"I met your friend Mr Wells," he continued. "He said the next time I had you in the chair and you couldn't answer back, I was to tell you not to give up writing about cricket."

Working with Bomber was such fun.

The next book I published was a collection of essays by David Foot, *Fragments of Idolatry*. As always with David, there was plenty of mental torment and suicide.

I don't know what David had actually said to Bomber. Bomber had a way of slightly reconstructing these things. But it was reported on to me that David had said that he enjoyed funerals. I think I knew what he meant. A funeral is a moment of standing still, when everything seems to have a heightened reality, a greater sense of perspective. For all the sadness people can be at their warmest at funerals.

I gave Bomber a copy of *Fragments*, and in exchange he offered me a handbill. "Here," he said with a grin. "Give this to your friend David. He might like to go along."

It was an advertisement for an open day at the local funeral directors.

Bomber's story was what county cricket should be all about. An ordinary lad growing up with no great advantages in life. Some early years in club cricket in his home town. Then the step up to play for the county. He had such great feeling for Gloucestershire, too, and he captured that beautifully when the following year we got together to write a foreword to a little book about the county's cricketers.

As always he sat in the big chair, now a motorised thing that could tip him forward and back, and I sat at right angles to him on the sofa. I suggested that he started with the county itself before going on to the cricket, and he was soon in full flow, his vowels at their broadest for the occasion.

'Glorious Gloucestershire. Is there another county of such beauty? The stone-built cottages snuggling in the Cotswold hills. The magical villages hidden in the ancient Forest of Dean. The mighty River Severn with its elvers. The town of Cheltenham: "poor, pretty and proud," as my dad used to say. And my own beloved Gloucester, with its majestic cathedral and its throbbing industrial heart. The Wagon Works, Moreland's Matches, Fielding and Platt. And overlooking the city, Robinswood Hill, where we used to picnic on a Sunday. A bottle of water, a few sandwiches, and we were away and happy the whole day long. Oh, the hours we spent sliding down that hillside.

I loved it. It did not take many months in Bomber's company for me to believe that Wally Hammond was the greatest cricketer ever. I even took out life membership of the club.

In 1959 the Gloucestershire captaincy passed from George Emmett to Tom Graveney, and Bomber lost his place to David Allen. Perhaps Tom wanted a little more batting and fielding than Bomber offered; perhaps he did not want the antics.

Bomber always reckoned that he could have killed off David Allen's career if he'd been so minded. "Emmett asked me one day what I thought of him. If I'd have said he wasn't good enough, he'd have been on his way. But I've always helped people. And I was content to play for anyone. It didn't matter if it was a Club and Ground game or the first team."

In 1958 David Allen had played seven championship matches and taken just two wickets. Five years had passed since that glorious afternoon when, as a 17-year-old, he had bowled out the great Surrey side at Bristol, taking six for 13 and being chaired off by his friends from school. He was getting nowhere, and he was ready to pack it in. But Colonel Henson, the Secretary, persuaded him to stay one more year, and such was the advance he made that summer that in August he was selected to play for England.

Bomber played in the second eleven, where his 87 wickets in 12 matches helped Gloucestershire to win the first ever second eleven championship. With Emmett deputising for Tom Graveney as first team captain, Bomber captained the majority of the games, too. "I'm still the only man who's captained the county to a championship," he would say.

He played only one first team game in 1959, taking six wickets at Trent Bridge. During the match the Notts coach, Frank Shipston, asked if he would join the staff there.

Sam Cook told him not to accept. Trent Bridge was the best batting track in the country, and Cook still associated it with the failure of his one and only Test cap: nought for 127 in 30 overs in 1947. "What do you want to go up there for, Bomb? You'll end up being cannon fodder."

Bomber had a different set of priorities. He liked the challenge of bowling on good pitches, and even more he liked Trent Bridge. "The apple and pear trees, the flower boxes on the balcony, the little hut where the ladies used to sell their home-made cakes. You could get there early, read the paper, have a cup of tea and a cake. And the lunches were marvellous, not like the little salads we used to have every day at Bristol, one slice of cold meat so thin you could see through it."

He wanted me to write a book with him about his later days in Nottingham. He gave me a manuscript 'The Bridge of Sighs', 76 pages that Mary had typed up some years earlier, and we did have a couple of sessions.

"Trent Bridge was like a palace compared with Bristol. In the changing rooms they had about three baths, where all we had at Bristol was a thing like a horse trough. Then at the end of the first month, when I got my pay, I went to the Secretary. I thought they'd paid me two months by mistake."

Gloucester was a city, but Nottingham was a big city, with three times the population. Bomber and his first wife Pat, who died while they were still up there, could tell the difference.

"On the pavement we got in the way because we were slow. In Gloucester people would take their time. We'd stop and sniff the air of the coffee grinding machine on the Cross, things like that. But in Nottingham they were all rushing around. All these stepping asides and knocking into people, it took us a while to realise we were the cause of it. They must have been walking two miles an hour faster than us. In a year or two, though, we were walking at their pace. Then, if we got back to Gloucester, everybody was so slow. It used to irritate us."

Notts were a poor bowling team, and Bomber bowled overs galore: 131 in his first two matches. "The ball did turn at Trent Bridge. That's the amazing thing. The old groundsman said to me, 'What do you think of bowling on it?' I said, 'It's quite good. It bounces and turns.' He was really quite offended."

He took 120 wickets in 1960. Then 99 in 1961, with – so he liked to describe – several dropped catches on the last day. But, best of all, in 1963 his 97 wickets included one that was special: Arthur Milton.

Arthur had explained to me how Bomber's bowling was faster than you expected, with the ball pitching further up. "He used to get people playing back to him, and the ball would be on them before they had time." Arthur played mainly off the back foot, but he told Bomber, "You'd never get me out. I wouldn't go back to you."

Arthur got to 49 against Notts at Cheltenham. "He was pushing, pushing, pushing forward," Bomber said. "Then I held this one back. And he pushed forward. He was plumb in front. It turned and was going to hit middle-and-off. He smiled and walked off. I did 'Gravy' the same at Trent Bridge."

Bomber had some lovely stories about his Nottingham days. One was about a fielder trying to retrieve a ball from an Alsatian dog at Bath: "Every time he went to pick up the ball, it bared its teeth and snarled. In the end they signalled four and got another ball. After that the crowd really took to Roger. Whenever the ball came near him, they all started barking."

Then there was a story about somebody being tricked into using a bat that was stuffed with compressed sawdust, how in a magnificent innings this chap had left a large pile of sawdust in the batting crease, and how the opposing keeper had inspected it with bewilderment. Bomber had written it up as an article in *The Cricketer*, supposedly as a tribute to the batsman, but the chap had sent him a solicitor's letter threatening a libel action.

It was hard to know what was true sometimes with Bomber.

"We thought he talked a load of rubbish when he first joined us," the amiable John Clay told me. "But whenever we looked into his stories, there always turned out to be more truth in them than we'd thought."

I couldn't get the book to work. Nottinghamshire had so few front-line players in those years, there wasn't the romance of the local boy playing for his own county, and I'd already written up so many of Bomber's views on cricket and life. So, despite several resolutions to get down to it, the book was never written.

I still occasionally find new references to him in match reports in the local newspapers. One in the *Yorkshire Post* described him batting at Sheffield:

> Twenty-five minutes of survival meant 32 invaluable runs for Gloucestershire and lively entertainment for the spectators who could appreciate a willing spirit and the humour of the game. Tail-enders do not customarily drive Trueman through the covers in the midst of a running conversation.

Another was from the *Bristol Evening Post*:

> The personality whom everybody missed, of course, was the one and only Bomber Wells. I gather that, as a result of the latest eccentricities, he is now rusticating in the 2nd XI. In a recent match he sent to the pavilion for his cap, put it on to bowl and then solemnly handed it back to the umpire at the end of each over.

In his heyday he was a hilarious after-dinner speaker, capable of reducing large audiences to continuous belly-aching laughter, though I never saw him. He had given all that up by the time I met him, and there was no question of his returning to it after he had had the stroke.

He started to recommend me as a speaker. Quite why, I don't know. My first engagement was at Trent Bridge, to the Nottingham Cricket Lovers Society, which he had founded in 1970. Their first speaker had been Garry Sobers, and now they had me. The chairman, seeing how nervous I was, gave me a little advice: "Try to work in Derek Randall. He's a great favourite up here." As my subject was county cricket in the 1950s, that was not easy. But Bomber seemed pleased with the feedback he got from them, and he found me some more opportunities.

Once his book had come out, I found the speaking easier. He had passed me the torch for telling his stories, and many of them were perfect for acting out: "'Come in from further back,' Sir Derrick said. So Bomber went back ten yards. And he bowled it from there."

I never miss the opportunity to tell one about a game he played for the Gloucester Nondescripts at Witney:

> "They had this chap Len Hemming. He played for Oxfordshire. Wonderful player. Well, I came off my one-pace run, and I bowled him. And, as he was going off, Bill Hook said to our skipper Jack Stevens, 'I don't think he was looking when Bomber bowled him. I'll get him to come back.' We played all away matches, you see, and we didn't like to offend anyone. So he came back rather sheepishly, and I bowled him next ball as well. And everyone started laughing. Well, Bill turned to Jack Stevens again. But before he could say a word, Len Hemming swung round. 'Bill, if you think I'm staying here for him to get his bloody hat-trick ….'"

Making people laugh, it's one of the greatest gifts – and Bomber had it.

In some ways he could be quite a selfish man. He liked things to revolve around him, and several of us worried that Mary was struggling, that he was taking her too much for granted. Ken Biddulph thought that strongly and was forever going up to Gloucester to "tell Bomber". But it made no difference. She would push the wheelchair everywhere, with his great weight in it, and he refused to get one he could drive himself.

Bomber's great strength was that he was cheerful, and he kept other people cheerful. I remember visiting him in the Gloucester Royal Infirmary one time. It could have been a depressing occasion, not helped by the non-stop gibberish the man in the bed opposite was talking. But Bomber only saw the funny side of it. "He's with the fairies," he said with a conspiratorial grin.

Yet there was a melancholy, as so often there is with comedians and romantics, even sometimes an anger. The first time I met him, I explained how I had started my writing with Ken Biddulph. "He's a lovely chap, isn't he?" I said. "He's still got so much enthusiasm for everything."

"Well, if you love the game," Bomber said, "you never lose that enthusiasm. It will dampen, but you'll never lose it. Ken's like me. Some of the goings on now, they're deplorable. The game's being run by conmen, basically."

Another time he was lamenting the decline of the spin bowler: "People now, they can't get to grips with the idea that a spinner is actually a devastating bowler if he bowls well, no matter what the wicket is like. Soon the generation will be gone who remember any different."

My own favourite came one day when he had slipped again into running down the modern game. "I don't know," he suddenly said. "Maybe, as you get older and you watch the young people playing, you start to have the wrong thoughts."

I loved the way he put that. 'You start to have the wrong thoughts.' It was so simple, yet so profound.

He loved watching cricket. Every Saturday in summer he would go to the Spa to see Gloucester City play. He would find midweek games where Mary would drive him and, when the Cheltenham Festival arrived, you could always find him in the corner beyond the main scoreboard, sitting with Mary and his great friend Norman, holding forth to whatever little gathering assembled around him. He could tell a non-stop stream of stories about the old days, but he would never miss anything that happened on the field, breaking off his stories to make comments about the field placings or the line of the bowling.

Towards the end, though, his speech got slower. The gatherings around him grew smaller, and his enthusiasm for the cricket did dampen. The wheelchair did not always help, either. He told me how he had got stuck all one afternoon with a statistician: "Every time I started a story, he'd get some book out of his bag and interrupt me, saying I'd got it all wrong. If I'd have been on my feet, I'd have walked away."

Statisticians, he did not like. He even pronounced the word with an awkward deliberateness, as if to emphasise that they were a pernickety bunch of buggers.

He said of Boycott, "He's given nothing to the game except facts and figures." That made me laugh. And he had a lovely story about retiring with 999 wickets: "Plenty of people have got a thousand, I bet no one's got 999," he said when he refused a further game. "Three months later some bloody statistician found I'd only got 998."

In truth, the inaccuracies in his stories were a problem. We live in an age of information, and people are less comfortable than they used to be with exaggeration. Heaven knows what sort of book the Bible would be if we wrote it today. Five loaves and two fishes feeding a crowd of five thousand? There would be statisticians and investigative journalists crawling all over the story.

Bomber belonged to an older tradition of oral story-telling. He did not only tell stories of George Emmett and Sam Cook, Roly Jenkins and Sir Derrick Bailey, he told them of Larwood and Voce, Hammond and Goddard, stories that had been told to him years earlier, stories that in some cases went back before the first world war.

"Charlie Parker told a lovely story about bowling at Ranjitsinhji. Ranji kept glancing him to leg. That was his shot, wasn't it? So Charlie went up to the captain – an amateur, Champain, I think – and he said, 'Excuse me, sir, do you think I could move second slip onto the leg-side to stop him doing that?' And Champain looked at him: 'Good God, man, are you trying to spoil the game?'"

I tried to look it up. I only found one game when Parker bowled to Ranji, and Ranji didn't make many runs. What's more, Champain, though he was playing, wasn't the captain. But that was missing the point of the story. It wasn't about filling in exact words spoken by exact people on exact dates. It was about telling me what the world of cricket was like in those days.

"When I started at Bristol," Bomber told me one time, "there was this old boy on the committee, Teddy Spry. As a young man he'd played with WG Grace. I used to sit with him. I think I was the only one who did. I loved listening to all his stories. You can learn a lot from old men, you know. They're the obvious people to ask. They might exaggerate things, but it doesn't matter. You get the gist of what they're trying to say."

I met Bomber for the last time in May 2008, on the first day of the county's match at the Archdeacon Meadow, the ground of the King's School in Gloucester. For one week each summer the county took their cricket to Bomber's home city, and the game was played in the shadow of the old cathedral. It had none of the splendour of Cheltenham College, and the crowds were not great. But Bomber supported it loyally, sitting always in the little enclosure where the groundsman parked his roller and mowing machine.

He was not in good form that day, and the cricket, after a bright morning, went downhill. The clouds came over, the Gloucestershire batting collapsed, and the players went off for bad light for a while. It was all a bit flat.

At the end of the day, as he was leaving, Bomber was sick. It was the last day's cricket he ever saw. He died in hospital three weeks later.

The next summer the accountants finally triumphed. For the first time since the 19th century, the county's fixture list did not include a match in Bomber's beloved Gloucester. I read the news, and I heard his voice in my head. Not an angry voice, I never heard him angry, but there was a hard edge to his debunking humour. "They were just waiting for me to die."

Bomber's funeral was at Gloucester Cathedral. He had no religious beliefs; his religion, such as it was, was the Labour Party, whom he stuck up for whatever they were doing. But he loved beautiful buildings and he had given so much help to the cricket at the King's School. So the cathedral, though it wasn't quite Bomber, had a certain appropriateness. It was also big enough to house the great crowd that attended.

Mary asked me to give the speech, and I spent three days writing and rewriting it. I wanted to tell a few of his best stories, so I worked in the chap at Hove with the little umbrella: "That man there will get someone killed." The Alsatian dog at Bath: "After that, the crowd really took to Roger. Whenever the ball came near him, they all started barking." Sir Derrick Bailey at Worcester: "Because that's what he actually said. Come in from further back." Even the game at Witney: "If you think I'm staying here for him to get his bloody hat-trick …" One more time I wanted them all to laugh with him.

I also wanted to capture something of his deeper feelings:

> Cricket was the great love that joined up everything in his life: from his childhood games in wartime in New Street to that last day we saw him in public, on the first day of the festival here in Gloucester. The pleasures he found in cricket ran deeper than the runs on the scoreboard, deeper than the winning and the losing of the game. For Bryan, cricket was an art form as much as a sport. It revealed all the richness of our humanity, our humour, our individuality. And on a sunny day at Cheltenham, when he was settled in that corner beyond the scoreboard, it provided him with a glimpse of eternity beyond our own short lives.

It was a disaster. Nobody laughed, nobody even smiled or looked happy. It was all wrong. I had struck the wrong tone. Bomber's irreverent humour did not belong in a cathedral.

It was only afterwards I discovered that nobody had heard any of it. My voice, amplified by a microphone, had bounced up into the vaulted roof and the words had jumped around till they were just an ugly cacophony.

"I tried putting in the hearing loop," Tom Graveney said. "I even tried shaking it and hitting it."

For some days afterwards I felt terrible. Then I thought of Bomber. I imagined him looking down on me from above: this chap at the lectern taking it all so seriously, sweating away as he talked nineteen to the dozen at the top of his voice. And not a soul could hear a word of what he was saying.

Bomber would have found it hilarious.

I still see Mary from time to time. There's a great gap in her life now.

On my last visit I asked her if her back was better for not having to push Bomber everywhere.

"No," she replied. "As a matter of fact, it's worse. And you know what, he always used to say how he was keeping me fit."

We laughed.

With Bomber the laughter was never far away.

Dickie Dodds and Sonny Avery

Ilford, 1949

5

DICKIE DODDS

If you prefer it religious

Thomas Carter Dodds

Born: Bedford, 29 May 1919

Died: Cambridge, 17 September 2001

"I've written out some notes on the players and the game. It will save us both a lot of time."

They were almost the first words Dickie Dodds spoke to me when we settled down in the front room of his modern house in St Neots, near Huntingdon. He had a slightly high-pitched, upper-class, insistent voice. He handed me ten typed pages. I looked at them, and my heart sank.

I didn't want him to give me his memories in the controlled language of written prose; I wanted his natural voice to flow freely out of conversation.

"Excellent," I said bravely. "But perhaps, as I've come all this way, we could have a little talk as well."

I sensed that he was somewhat suspicious of me, and particularly of my tape recorder, but he agreed to go ahead – though on the telephone he had needed my reassurance that I would show him what I wrote and that he could remove anything he did not like.

He had been recommended to me by his Essex captain Doug Insole. I had had occasion to ring Doug when I was researching Arthur Milton's game, and I asked him who at Essex would be a good person to interview.

"Preferably somebody with a good sense of humour," I suggested.

"Well, if you like your humour bucolic, you could try Tonker Taylor. Or if you'd prefer it religious, there's Dickie Dodds."

For some reason, perhaps because I liked the idea of something different, I opted for the religion.

"I thought cricket was a ridiculous occupation," Dickie said. "In the winter I would be changing the course of history. Then in the summer I had to get back to cricket. I had to keep telling myself that this was what God wanted me to be doing."

It was a strange conversation, sometimes quite strained. He had one agenda, to proselytise on behalf of the Moral Rearmament movement, and I had another, to learn about county cricket in the 1950s. He wanted to challenge my outlook on life, and half of me wanted to rise to that challenge. The other half, however, wanted to stick with questions about his Essex team-mates and the game he had chosen as his most memorable.

The game was at Brentwood in June 1952. On the final day Lancashire set Essex 232 to win in two hours 20 minutes, and Dickie faced the first ball of the innings from Brian Statham.

"He didn't try to hit you. Other bowlers, they tried to hit you, and you knew they were trying to hit you. He'd bowl you bouncers, yes, but that was a technical thing. You were playing cricket with him; you weren't trying to stop him knocking your teeth out."

When I got home, I found I needed the typed sheets to tell me what happened next:

> 'I hooked his first ball for four. I pulled his next ball for six. As I ran to the bowler's end, Brian looked slightly puzzled. "Hey, Dick," he said. "What's going on?" Anyway, that was ten off two balls.'

"Our characters are reflected in the way we play," he explained. "You'll never hit the first ball for six if you've never thought of it. So you play the way you think, and you choose the way you play. You may not have thought you have chosen it, but you have."

He started to elaborate his thesis, and it was some while before we returned to Brentwood. He told me how in later years he had taken to questioning cricketers about their motivations. His first example was Ken Barrington, whose England average of 58.67 remains the highest of all among post-war batsmen.

"I was having dinner one night with him, and I posed this question. And he was straight out. 'I'll tell you why I played. I decided after a year or two in cricket that I was going to be a success. Success meant runs. It meant how many runs you got at the end of the season and what your average was. So I decided I was going to get as many runs as possible, regardless of how I got them.' And he got a lot of runs. Personally I wouldn't have crossed the street to watch him bat. But that was his aim and his philosophy."

He went on to talk about Wilf Slack, the West Indian born batsman who – at the time of meeting Dickie in 1981 – had been on the Middlesex staff for several years without ever establishing himself.

"His change was the most dramatic of any I had anything to do with. He was 26. He'd never got more than 60 runs in his life in a first-class match, and we were talking a bit like we're talking now. I didn't know him from Adam. But three or four days later he said to me, 'Can you tell me a bit more about this motivation?' And I looked at him and I thought, 'That chap will understand. So I gave him my message."

The conversation took place at Lord's during the second Test of 1981, with Wilf Slack not even in the Middlesex side.

"That was Botham's last Test as captain. Brearley got picked for the next Test. Slack got picked in Brearley's place for Middlesex. And he got 180 not out. And the next match he got 230 not out. He got a thousand runs in a month."

I looked it up in *Wisden*, and it was pretty accurate: 56 and 181 not out against Kent, then 4 and 248 not out against Worcestershire. Between July 15 and August 14 he scored 1,011 runs.

"Then he stopped getting runs, and I knew what had happened. He'd gone back on his decision. So I went to see him. I said, 'Look, are you now playing to get in the England side, Wilf?' He said, 'I can't help it. Everybody's talking about it. It's in all the papers.' I said, 'Rubbish. You can help it. You choose your motivation. Nobody chooses it for you.' He changed again, and he did play for England."

Dickie reached into his jacket pocket to produce a little note book where he had written down some words that Ian Botham had spoken to an interviewer after one of his great hundreds in 1981: 'You've got to enjoy it, let it go, let it speak for itself, let it take you over. You've got to set it free and not get in its way.'

"You know," a priest had said to Dickie. "That's a perfect expression of the Holy Spirit."

I had grown up a Methodist. The Sermon on the Mount resonated with me, and the verse about the rich man and the camel passing through the eye of a needle. But I had never till that moment understood the Holy Spirit.

"It's what's inside you that matters," Dickie continued. "It's how you stop fear, jealousy, ambition blocking you."

He told me of a Test match – in India, I think – when, during a break in play, he bumped into one of the *Test Match Special* team.

"Hello, Dickie, we knew you were on the ground. We've just been talking about you on air."

"Oh? What have you been saying?"

"We've been speculating on which England cricketer you would have most chance of converting to Moral Rearmament."

"Oh?"

"And we all came up with the same answer."

"Who was that?"

"Ian Botham."

Dickie had written a book about his life, *Hit Hard And Enjoy It*. I had read it the previous day and found it utterly absorbing. It was part autobiography, part statement of faith, part elegy for the rhythm of English county cricket's summer. In it he described his war service in India, when he had led the social life of a young blade, and the discussions they had had in the officers' mess about the better world they were going to build when the war was over. One officer, an architect, preached communism; another, a doctor, belonged to the Moral Rearmament movement. Both ideas had their attractions for Dickie, but he watched the two men closely and he made his decision.

'I found the architect to be full of bitterness, fear and a consuming personal ambition. I said to myself that an idea and philosophy that did not deal with these things in people would not do what is necessary in the world. When I came to look closely at the doctor's life I found he had a freedom in such matters. I became convinced that his ideas were the right ones because they dealt with the root of the trouble: the wrong things in people which led to all the other wrongs.'

Dickie was born Thomas Carter Dodds in May 1919. He was the son of a country parson, growing up in a rambling vicarage in Bedfordshire, where the gardener spent many hours bowling to him. He attended Wellingborough School, where he played on the first eleven, and after school, drifting through office jobs, he played a few games of county second eleven cricket, first for Warwickshire, then for Middlesex. At this stage he was a leg-break bowler who batted well down the order.

He played wartime cricket in India, and he still harboured hopes of being a cricketer when he was demobbed in the spring of 1946. But Middlesex were no longer interested in him, and he found himself catching a train to Chelmsford for a trial with Essex. At the nets he bowled his leg breaks, soon realising that there were several there who bowled them better than he did. Then, at the end of the session, he was astonished to be told, "You're just the man we need to open the batting."

By then he had converted to Moral Rearmament, and he prayed to God for guidance. The voice that came back said, 'Hit hard and enjoy it.'

"The highest form of prayer I knew," he told me, "was to play beautiful shots for a creator who loved beautiful things. My job was to give recreation to those who came to watch. Re-creation. Lift their spirits. I believe that we can all find re-creation when we glimpse creativity. But if what we see is materialism, it will be dull."

In Dickie's scheme of things Ken Barrington had allowed himself to become an acquisitive materialist, where others played with a freer spirit:

Denis Compton: "He was the most creative player I ever saw. A remarkable person. I found him as entertaining off the field as on." Brian Lara: "When he hit that 375, he loved to hit the ball. He had no fear, only love. Garry Sobers was the same." Harold Gimblett: "As high strung as you like but, boy, what a creative player!" The Kent leg-spinner Doug Wright: "The most creative bowler I ever saw. He tried to bowl the best ball every time. Other bowlers bowled the percentage."

All his examples were of cricketers who were not afraid to attack, who expressed themselves dynamically. So I asked him if he could think of anybody who passed his test of creativity who was a quieter, calmer character. He thought for a long time, but he gave no reply.

"I feel cricket can be so deadly dull," he went on. "If you bowl one ball, there are about four shots you can try to play to it. But so many people play like automata."

"And one-day cricket? Does that create more improvisation?"

No, I was still not tuned in thoroughly to his thinking.

"What is communicated to the spectators?" he asked. "I don't see them excited by an art form. It's a lower level. The excitement is because someone's got to win, that's all. 3.2 an over, 4.6 an over. It's an accountant's day out. I don't see their spirits revived or re-created."

The game at Brentwood built to a superb climax. When the last over began, Essex needed nine runs for victory, and their last pair were at the crease: Trevor Bailey, on strike, and Frank Vigar, a good enough batsman to have scored 1,700 runs one year but who, like Bailey, had been dropped down the order to allow the quicker run-scorers to have a go first.

Nine to win, one over to be bowled by Lancashire's slow left-armer Malcolm Hilton. And Dickie keen to tell me how you played the way you thought, how motivation was the key to it all.

What happened next did not join the pieces of the jigsaw together, and it all hinged on the character of Trevor Bailey.

"Bailey to me was an enigma," Dickie said. "I expect I was to him. I couldn't fathom him. Whatever it was that drove him, I never found it. I still don't know. He was a complete mystery."

The first ball was sent down, and Bailey met it with an immaculate forward defensive. The following summer he would become 'Barnacle Bailey', saving a Test against Australia at Lord's with four and a quarter hours of such defensive play. His patience became legendary.

The second ball was sent down, seemingly no different from the first, and he unleashed a lofted off-drive that sent the ball high over the far boundary for six. Dickie's written notes elaborated the moment:

> 'We could not believe our eyes. Excited cheers from the crowd were followed by chattering as neighbours exclaimed on the astonishing phenomenon they had just witnessed. Three runs from four balls were wanted. We could get them in singles. Now was the time for Bailey to play his famous forward push into the gap.'

But did Bailey play it? No. He launched into another lofted off-drive, and the ball this time went higher and less far, landing in the hands of long-off. Dickie was at something of a loss to explain it. But the groans turned into cheers as the fielder spilled the catch and the batsmen completed a second run. Scores were level, and there were three balls left.

I had such fun writing it up. I found a quote in a coaching book by Trevor Bailey: 'The one thing that the batsman must avoid is to lose his head. ... He must avoid having a death or glory swing.'

Then I found a description of the next ball, the fourth of the over, in the *Brentwood Gazette*: Astonishingly Trevor Bailey, rather than pushing the ball safely into a gap, launched the same lofted off-drive a third time.

> 'Over two thousand sun-drenched cricket lovers let loose a yell that was thrown skywards and must have reverberated throughout the county. They were all of one opinion that Trevor Bailey had made the winning hit. But he hadn't. Nigel Howard, the Lancashire captain, scooped the ball from nowhere, and the game was tied.'

Forty-five years had passed, and Dickie Dodds, sitting comfortably in his arm chair, was still mystified.

"I don't know why he did it. I don't think he knows why he did it. He claimed he didn't know what the score was. But Bailey who always knew everything about everything, Bailey forgotten what the score was, that was ridiculous."

"What was said afterwards? Did you talk about it?"

"We didn't have very serious sessions in the dressing room. You couldn't have a serious session with Insole around."

"Presumably he'd hit straight sixes before?"

"I'd never seen him hit one."

Dickie's typed notes expressed the view that for the third ball 'the cheers seemed to have gone to Trevor's head' and for the fourth: 'Alas Trevor's delight in this new batting abandon had taken over completely.'

I was in utter confusion. I had spent an hour and more, trying to keep up with Dickie's wonderfully stimulating views on playing cricket, how you need to rid yourself of fear and acquisitive materialism, how you should let it all go, set yourself free, and here he was, shaking his head in horror at the memory of Trevor Bailey – "Bailey of all people" – attempting to win a match by hitting ball after ball for six, when all he had to do was play the percentage and prod a single.

He turned the pages of the relevant *Wisden*, and he pointed out that in the previous match, also at Brentwood, Essex won by two wickets with three minutes to spare. Then in the following game, amid the rhododendrons at Tunbridge Wells, a young amateur Colin Griffiths hit the fastest century of 1952. There was a Brighter Cricket award that summer, sponsored by the *News Chronicle*, and Essex were its winners.

"These three matches are of the spirit in which we played our cricket. Because that spirit went, they tried to legislate to make people play the game the way it should be played."

A few days later I tracked down Colin Griffiths, and he spoke to me on the telephone. He said that Dickie had got it wrong. Trevor was not the Barnacle at that time; all that began the following year. "He could be impetuous. I don't think at that stage that he'd really worked out his batting role. A year or so later he'd never have played that last over the way he did. He was a very difficult man to understand, very difficult to put in any box."

I have thought about it a lot in the years since, and I have often wondered if the ambiguities of the English class system might have had something to do with Dickie's reaction to Trevor Bailey.

Dickie came from a well-established English family. In an earlier age he would have been an amateur, but he lacked the means in that post-war world and he played as a professional. Just as Paul Gibb, the Essex wicket-keeper, did, though he too had 'a good background', had been to Cambridge and played as an amateur till 1946. It was simply not done for a university man to play his cricket as a professional and, when Gibb made the switch, he had to forfeit his membership of MCC.

Trevor Bailey, by contrast, came from more humble origins, but his sporting prowess allowed him unusually to attend prep and public school, followed by Cambridge University. At Essex, in order that he could play as an amateur, he was offered the rather nebulous post of Assistant Secretary.

Who was he? Where had he come from? Why did he know everything? He was, indeed, 'an enigma', 'very difficult to put in any box'.

At one stage Dickie's choice of most memorable match was going to be one against Middlesex at Leyton in 1957. His benefit match. It was the county's return to the East End after 24 years, it saw Denis Compton's penultimate first-class century and Essex turned round a heavy first-innings deficit to win a famous victory. But he had written about it at length in his book so I steered him away to Brentwood.

Most beneficiaries insured their matches against rain, but Dickie chose to pray – and he was rewarded with three days of warm sunshine. At the end of it he decided to give all the money to Moral Rearmament.

> 'Before I left the ground, a small boy approached me. I thought
> he wanted an autograph. Instead, he stood there looking up at me:
> "Wot yer going to do wiv all that money, Dick?" he asked. Truth
> to tell, I hadn't thought. I found myself saying, "I'm going to use
> it to help build a new world." "Cor!" he said.'

When Mrs Thatcher was Prime Minister, he took a copy of his book to Downing Street, handing it in with a letter drawing her attention to the passages about communism and Christianity, about the perils of materialism and the importance of individual choice. The next day her principal private secretary rang.

"Mrs Thatcher wants to thank you very much for the book. She wants to know if she should sign it and send it back."

"All I wanted," Dickie replied, "is for her to read chapters five and six."

"Oh," he said. "I'll do the best I can."

Dickie was a member of the Conservative Party, living in John Major's Huntingdon constituency. I put it to him that you could argue, in terms of his Moral Rearmament philosophy, that Mrs Thatcher's policies – with their emphasis on material gain as the driving force of human progress – were just as lacking in a spiritual dimension as the communism he had spent his life opposing.

"Materialism of the left and materialism of the right are two sides of the same coin. That's why I sent her this blessed book."

I think he knew she had not read it, but I did. Several times. There are three beautiful chapters on Essex's summer-long journey around England, ending with the last benefit matches in September:

> 'As you stood in the cricket field of a club like Epping you could sense the strain of the county round oozing out of you. It was a wonderful relaxing feeling in the stillness and warmth of a late summer's afternoon. You and nature were at one. … It was a time of fruit-gathering and blackberrying. The swallows had left for their winter quarters and soon, in a day or so, would you.'

There is not another book like it.

I have known a number of people of my own generation who have been attracted to cult groups of one sort or another – mostly religious or political – and I could see the things they had in common with Dickie. At one point he started to talk to me about the radio and television waves that are all around us in the atmosphere, how we have no idea what effect they are having on us. He spoke as if it were a great, hidden conspiracy of evil powers. Part of me was in full agreement with him, ready to sign up to some great campaign; another part said, 'Don't go down that road. Just rub along with the crowd in normal society.'

"Dodds is almost an anachronism," the *Playfair Annual* for 1953 wrote. "He should be knighted for his spirit of adventure."

Doug Insole put it differently in his autobiography: "His appearance is sufficiently dignified to qualify him for a bishopric, the Cabinet, or a television panel game while his batting is fit for a World Eleven or the madhouse."

For many of the other professionals, his religion was a source of both amusement and bewilderment. "When he's got the message," Somerset's Arthur Wellard would complain, "there's no bowling at this bugger."

Dickie's later opening partner, the Yorkshireman Gordon Barker, was scratching around one day while Dickie was blazing away. "I think God's shown him the light," one fielder quipped, and back came Barker's reply: "Well, I wish he'd get Him to shine some of it down this bloody end."

Eventually I got Dickie to talk about his team-mates, and he started with Paul Gibb. "When he was small, he wanted to be heavyweight boxing champion of the world. Then he got glandular fever or rheumatic fever, and he never grew much after that. His doctor said he had a bad heart, he mustn't do anything energetic, so he took up squash, tennis and cricket."

He talked about the all-rounder Ray Smith, whose double of 1,000 runs and 100 wickets in 1947 came from the prodigious workload of 55 innings and 1,557 overs. "He came off the farm in April, he never did any press-ups or laps, he smoked like a chimney and he was never injured. He loved cricket. It was a calling for him. He didn't play it for money."

This led him back to the theme of motivation.

"Two pounds for a win, one pound for a draw. To me it was an insult. Ridiculous. Would Ray Smith bowl any harder because there was two pounds for a win? Of course he wouldn't. Money is not an adequate motive. You've got to love cricket."

Dickie's greatest affection was reserved for his opening partner in those years, Sonny Avery, a barber's son from East London whose early cricket had been up against a lamp post or in the park with a coat draped over a stick.

"He was an artist, a craftsman. In another age he would have been a great leather-worker – or a sculptor, carving beautiful things on churches."

Sonny was the only one who came to Dickie's Moral Rearmament meetings – "Ray Smith got as far as the door once" – and, though he was never recruited, he did join Dickie from time to time. They went to the assembly shop at Ford's Dagenham plant, they spoke to meetings in East Ham Town Hall and they visited the home of an East End revolutionary who kept a hand grenade on his mantelpiece. They even persuaded Sonny's mother, who distributed leaflets for the Communist Party, to attend a showing of the Moral Rearmament play 'The Forgotten Factor'. According to Dickie, she was 'radiant' when she came out.

Sonny gave his later life to coaching: first as captain of Gloucestershire Seconds, then at Monmouth School. "He loved seeing the craft, the skill, coming alive in a boy. I'm sure he was a wonderful coach. Sport was in him. He was impelled towards it. I really believe that almost everybody's got a destiny of one sort or another."

Monmouth was not far away so I telephoned Sonny Avery. His wife Marjorie answered, telling me that he was very poorly, close to death. But she suggested a time that I should come up.

Twice he was too ill to see me, and after the second cancellation I suggested that perhaps I should leave it. I was making a nuisance of myself. "No, he does want to see you," she insisted, and finally there was an afternoon when he was well enough for a visit.

He sat in the armchair. He was one of those people whose face told you straightaway that he was a nice man, and he tried very hard to answer my questions. He was clearly in pain but, speaking slowly, he recalled his days working as a clerk at Essex's Leyton headquarters in the early 1930s.

"The office was situated above the pavilion, looking straight down the wicket. When I should be working, I was watching – and that's where I learnt a lot, by watching. Patsy Hendren. I remember Patsy Hendren getting 200 at Leyton, and he never lifted the ball from the ground."

He told me of his debut at The Oval in 1935. "I was with Tom Wade at Chelmsford. The idea was to help the groundsman in the morning and to practise in the afternoon. But how could we practise? Tom was a wicket-keeper, and I was a batsman. This girl called me. 'Come along,' she said. 'You're playing at The Oval tomorrow.' I thought she was pulling my leg."

He scored 28 not out in the first innings, batting at number nine. But his memory was sharper when he recalled his second innings.

"I didn't last very long. Alf Gover got me out for a duck, caught at the wicket. The following season I was promised I would play in every game. In actual fact I played none."

I made the mistake of butting in. I wanted to know if anything was said that summer, about his not playing. Did people in those days talk to you about such things? Or were you just left to cope on your own?

He paused for ages. I had broken the flow of his thought, and he struggled to find some way of answering my question. Eventually he spoke: "It's such a long time ago to remember a detail like that."

"We always told him he should write a book," Marjorie said. "He had so many lovely stories."

I wrote up the chapter, called it 'The Bailey Enigma' and sent it to Dickie. A few days later it was returned like a school essay, covered with crossings-out and amendments. There were 24 in all, each of them accompanied by a lengthy justification.

There were places where he felt he had been unfair to Trevor Bailey: "Tape recorders are dangerous things; I am afraid I talked without thinking.' And he wanted to remove the passage about Ian Botham and the Holy Spirit: 'I don't think it would help Botham to have this in print. He would fear derision, I would think. It would help him backward rather than forward.'

I accepted most of his points, replying in detail, and we spent nearly four months sending the chapter back and forth till finally he approved it. 'There comes a time in the life of every manuscript,' he wrote, 'when you have to say Enough, this is it. It seems to me this point has been reached. Otherwise there is a danger that more fiddling and the thing goes downhill.'

By then Sonny Avery had died, and Dickie told me how he had driven across to see him one last time.

"He was in hospital, in a ward of eight men, all waiting to die. He was so ill I hardly recognised him. But gradually he focused on me as I sat by his bed, and he became more animated as we talked of old days in the sun. We began to laugh, as Essex players always seem to do, at the fun we had. I could ring him up, and it was just the same as if we saw each other every day. That's what Marjorie and Kathleen found so odd. You go through so much together, the ups and downs. Sonny used to say, he'd go up the back lane when he got nought – so he didn't have to meet the people in the street.

"We had a wonderful half hour together. I told him to remember that we all get a second innings. He looked at me and smiled. 'I only hope my next one is better than my last.' I prayed with him, and afterwards he gripped my arm and thanked me. I'll never forget it. Our partnership was somehow rounded off. On the way out of Monmouth I stopped at a garden centre and bought a small tree that I've planted in our garden in his memory."

My book, with its Brentwood chapter now called 'Hit Hard and Enjoy It', came out in late 1997. Dickie reported back to me that he had been to the Christmas reception of his local Conservative Association.

"Ah, Dickie," John Major said to him. "I've just been reading about you."

"He said it was the best book on cricket he'd read."

"The best?"

"Or one of the best. I can't remember exactly what he said. Certainly the word 'best' came into it."

By now Dickie had grown more easy with me.

Later that winter England were playing in the West Indies. In the final Test they were pressing to square the series, and an unlikely pair of West Indian openers took to hitting the quick bowlers back over their heads. It was like nothing you expected to see in Test cricket, and Caddick and Fraser looked utterly bemused.

A few days later a postcard from St Neots landed on my door mat.

'Three cheers for Lambert and Wallace,' it read.

The editor of *The Cricket Society Journal* invited me to write an article, and I settled on 'Dodds and Avery', the Essex opening pair from those early post-war years. So I returned to St Neots.

Dickie told me that this was the first house he had ever owned. He had lived an itinerant life, working for Moral Rearmament all over the world, and he had been left it by a fellow member.

He talked about his involvement in the conversion of Conrad Hunte, the West Indian opening batsman, and I found a passage in Hunte's autobiography about an inter-racial meeting in Birmingham in the late 1960s. Dickie – 'one of the most English of the English', Hunte called him – attended and made a speech:

> 'He got up quietly and said, "I owe many here an apology. I have come to realise that I have never considered that a coloured person could become a cabinet minister here – or even an M.P. I never thought of any of you having a position of real authority. I thought of you as doing certain kinds of work – work in subordinate positions. I am sorry for this arrogant attitude." You could have heard a pin drop. Such simple honesty has a healing quality which no legal process can possess.'

Dickie was more relaxed on this visit. He spent less time on his 'message', and he let himself talk freely about Sonny and about the first summer after the war, when he left the army and found himself summoned to Ilford to play Sussex. "I didn't even know where Ilford was." He made 18 and 63, but the runs became harder to score in the following games. "They didn't have a team sheet. It was all very casual. I didn't know what the drill was. You just tag along automatically. We played at Hove, and I didn't do well. My recollection is, I asked Tom Pearce at Victoria. 'Am I wanted in the next match?' And he said, 'Oh, yes, you're very much wanted.'"

They were times of great change for Dickie. Back to civilian life after nearly seven years in the Army. Living every day with this travelling band of cricketers. And inwardly working through the implications of his spring-time conversion to Moral Rearmament. Tom Wade, the wicket-keeper, had probed his secret out of him in the Ship Hotel, Brighton. "He noticed that I didn't drink. He was the straightest person I ever met, and he got it out of me." Some of his team mates were not impressed. "You can't play cricket unless you drink beer," they said. And off they all went to Brentwood, where he teamed up for the first time with Sonny Avery, back after six weeks out with a finger injury. Sonny, too, had been in India during the war, working with Toc-H.

They had two matches at Brentwood, and Sonny scored 102, 83 not out and 44. It was a time for English cricket to rebuild, to find new players, and at the end of the week he was selected for the Test trial at Canterbury in July, where he made 79 out of 175. "Avery played the bowling on its merits," *The Times* reported, "and made some of the other batting look rather poor stuff." He must have been so close to an England cap. "Oh no," he had told me. "I knew I wasn't good enough. I was out of my class really."

"Running through his life," Dickie reflected, "there was a sort of sadness that repeated itself over and over." The Test trial that did not see him picked, the finger injuries, his mother's sudden death, then later the murder of his daughter in an armed raid on the jewellers where she worked. "She only went in that week out of the goodness of her heart," Dickie said. "It made him wonder why, if there was a loving God, He allowed these things to happen."

At Brentwood Dickie made 5, 6 and 13, but he stayed in the team that went to The Oval, where by mid-afternoon on the first day Surrey were all out for 162 and he and Sonny were stepping out to bat. Dickie asked Sonny to take first strike. "If he did this," he remembered thinking, "at least I'd be in no danger of returning first ball to the pavilion." Such was the state of his confidence.

Alongside him Sonny was giving a first outing to a bat an Essex member had just given him. "It had belonged to this chap's son. I think perhaps he'd been killed in the war, and the father wanted Sonny to use it. That appealed to Sonny. He had that streak of sentiment."

The scoreboard was soon moving. "I can remember in that game, discovering how, if I dropped my left elbow when I played straight, the ball would go like a bullet to the mid-wicket boundary. I think it was Bedser, he was furious. If you drop your elbow at the point of impact, it'll turn the ball. I found myself observing it. 'Well, fancy that.' It kept happening."

At close of play they were 235 for no wicket.

"I bet you wish you could bat on this every day," a tired Alf Gover quipped to them as they left the field.

"Well, you all managed to get out on it," Dickie retorted.

That was Saturday evening, and on Monday morning they raised their partnership to 270. It remained the Essex first wicket record till 1994. At the start of the innings Dickie had declined first strike, aware only of the potential humiliation of returning first ball. Now he was being presented his county cap, heading off to Foster's in Bruton Street to order himself a blazer. And Sonny went on to his first double century.

"Sonny was a very calm, philosophical character. He was very much a thinking player. He thought far more about technique than I did. I didn't know how I played, but he would tell me."

Then came another of those mind-bending moments Dickie would produce: "You've got to love the game. If you don't love it, you begin to love the technique. And to love the technique is hopeless. Sonny loved cricket. He loved sport. He loved the game more than the technique."

I spoke again to Colin Griffiths. His own brief foray into county cricket had been a strange affair, the fastest hundred of 1952 and a lot of failures caused, he felt, by too much throwing of the bat in madcap run chases. He made some acerbic comments about two or three of the senior players – but not Sonny Avery. "Sonny was a lovely man. He never got involved in the politics. He and Dickie were a great partnership, as people as well as cricketers."

In 1947, still on the edge of England honours, Sonny suffered a broken finger and missed much of the summer. Dickie, by contrast, scored 2,147 runs and came close to selection for that winter's tour of West Indies. Winston Place of Lancashire won the last batting spot, and Dickie overcame his disappointment by saying to himself, "It was not what God wanted for me."

Dickie was not an accumulator of runs. In his career he turned only one in eight of his 50s into 100s, where for the more conventional Winston Place the figure was one in three. Yet Dickie's hard hitting frequently demoralised opposition attacks. In 1952, the summer of that Brentwood game, he scored 1,801 runs at a rate of 40 an hour. In all of England, only Colin Griffiths, with just 465 runs, scored faster.

When I left his house that afternoon he pointed me to a rose bed in his front lawn. There, planted in memory of Sonny, was a weeping cotoneaster. "There are white flowers in the spring," he told me, "followed by year-long red berries."

'Partners in Time', I called the *Cricket Society* article. It told the story of their great partnership at The Oval and of their last meeting in the hospital at Monmouth. It described Dickie's choice between communism and Christianity, and there was some recurring imagery involving trees: the lime at Canterbury and the blossom around the Brentwood boundary. There were also, threaded into the weave, some extracts from Eliot's 'Four Quartets'.

In my beginning is my end. Now the light falls
Across the field, leaving the deep lane
Shuttered with branches, dark in the afternoon.

I sent it to Dickie, who returned a brief note: 'Brilliant. It moved me. A local author who read it said, "What wonderful writing – who is this man?"'

That last line made me laugh.

And do you know what? There was not a sign of a correction.

You've got to enjoy it, let it go, let it speak for itself, let it take you over. You've got to set it free and not get in its way.

Dickie died in September 2001, but from time to time I still hear his insistent voice: challenging me, challenging the way I have come to see the world.

"When I was a boy," he told me, "cricket was a pleasurable activity. A game. You had a game of cricket. You didn't play in order to win. When I went home to my father, it wasn't a question of 'Who won?' It was 'Did you have a good game?' Now, with all this one-day cricket, the result has become the great thing. But there's more to cricket than the result."

He never tired of saying it.

"You have to love the game."

Eric Hill and Harold Gimblett
Taunton

6

ERIC HILL

Let's not get downhearted

Eric Charles Hill, D.F.C., D.F.M.

Born: Taunton, 9 July 1923

Died: Williton, 29 July 2010

The little village of Sampford Brett lies on the north-western edge of the Quantocks, a quiet corner of England where small hamlets are scattered among the farm fields and woodlands of the gentle rolling hills, where the lanes are narrow and the pace of life slow. I drove down the main street of the village, turned left – as instructed – at the post box on the telegraph pole and into a cul-de-sac. At the far end I found the bungalow, 'Pennypiece', where Eric Hill lived with his wife Dorothy. It was ten in the morning, a cold January day in 2000.

Another dispute was in progress between British farmers and the French government. They had invited me to stay for lunch and, when I offered on the telephone to bring a bottle of wine, Eric had responded immediately: "As long as it's not French." We were a long way from city life, a long, long way from New Labour territory.

"As a kid I had assumed my first appearance at Lord's would be opening the innings for England. With Len Hutton. That was how I would first appear at Lord's."

There was a tiny study beyond the living room, and we sat in there. In the bookcase I spotted some volumes on aircraft and the Second World War alongside the *Wisdens* and other cricket titles. There was also a photograph of Eric walking out to bat for Somerset alongside the great Harold Gimblett.

"In actual fact, I made my first appearance at Lord's on February the 16th, 1942. With a slight sleet falling and snow on the ground. Signing on for the RAF. The swearing officer insisted on saying each time, 'King George the Sixth, his Hairs and Successors,' and none of us could stop giggling. The most solemn moment of our lives. We did the signing in the Long Room. It was bloody cold."

He returned to Lord's on Saturday 10 May 1947. It was a much warmer day, and he was making his debut for Somerset. It was the first match of the summer, the first for Somerset under the captaincy of the eccentric Millfield headmaster RJO Meyer.

"The previous day we were in the old pavilion at Taunton. In the amateur dressing room; there was more room in there. RJO had a piece of paper, and we were instructed to get into our positions as if we were in the field. 'Bertie's on at this end, making 'em boom a bit ... Does everybody know where they are? ... Right. That's the end of Bertie, now it's Arthur.' And we all had to swap round for Arthur at the other end. 'Good. Now it's Tremmy.' The old 'uns all thought it was a load of rubbish."

Legion are the stories of RJO. He ran Millfield on Robin Hood principles: getting the wealthy to pay more so that he could take in children of sporting ability from poorer homes. On the cricket field he was full of eccentric theories, bewildering the professionals with requests to swipe the first ball for four or bowl a leg-side full-toss. On an express train to Manchester he once pulled the communication cord, bringing the train to a juddering halt, in order to request some food for the players. He gulped down aspirins to cope with bad lumbago, and at The Oval one day he suddenly exclaimed, "My feet are killing me", put his boots behind the stumps and fielded in socks. "He shouldn't have played," Eric said, "but everybody was frightened to tell him."

Ken Biddulph told me how a few years later the Somerset side used to play a pre-season game against Millfield. "He always insisted we had to take the full first eleven, and he'd have 22 in his team. He'd only field eleven at a time, but he'd have all these fast bowlers and a green wicket. Two of them would have a spell. Then he'd send them off and bring two more on. On one occasion he bowled us all out for 120 or so. And, of course, all 22 of them batted. And they beat us. They lost 19 wickets, and they beat us. He was going round telling everybody, 'My boys have beaten Somerset.'"

"I don't think he made himself understood sufficiently with people," Eric said more sympathetically. "He used to take teams round, playing schools. The first time he got me to play, he said, 'Eric, I'd like you to open the innings for me, and I'd like you to make a hundred. Show the lads how to bat.' 'I'll do my best,' I said. And I made a hundred. 'Thank you,' he said. 'Now you go and buy yourself a bat and send me the bill.' Another time we were at Clifton College. He was experimenting with a new bowling grip, and he had me diving around at short leg. 'You go and buy yourself a new pair of trousers,' he said at the end."

The fielding drill in the amateur dressing room was completed, the players caught the train to London and on a sunny Saturday morning everything went smoothly for a while. Arthur Wellard trapped Sid Brown lbw, Eric's fellow debutant Maurice Tremlett bowled Jack Robertson and, best of all, Bertie Buse dismissed Denis Compton when he had only scored six. "Then this chap comes in. Eaglestone. He hadn't played before. We didn't know him and, when he took guard, he was left-handed. And the old pros, they all just stood there. Dear old Jack Meyer. It took him ages to sort it out. It was total chaos."

Eric played for Somerset for five years, with only moderate success, but he went on to be a journalist, covering the county's cricket for the next forty years, and I took to him straightaway. He shone with integrity, and he told things as he saw them, all with that uncomplicated Somerset way of talking. He had an excellent memory, a keen ear for conversation and a sharp eye on human frailties. The characters and scenes came alive in my head when he talked about them.

He was particularly good on his opening partner, Harold Gimblett. "A very difficult man. A funny light-and-darkness sort of bloke. Sometimes he'd be all fun, mixing in with the boys, having a beer. Another time he'd not be talking to anybody, which of course didn't go down very well with that lot: people like Arthur Wellard, who'd put up with anything."

So many roads at Somerset led back to Harold Gimblett: to his astonishing century on debut at Frome, to his years of brilliance at the top of the batting order, to his depressions, his electro-convulsive treatment and eventual suicide. David Foot wrote movingly about him, calling him 'the tormented genius of cricket', but Eric saw it in more down-to-earth terms.

Gimblett was a boy from Bicknoller, the next village down from Sampford Brett. In the feudal hierarchy of the countryside, his family always wanted to seem a little higher up the scale than they were. They ran the pub at one time, laying on a Christmas party for the villagers, only to put on the bottom of the notice: 'No labourers'.

Eric reckoned Gimblett "exploited this stress thing; he got in when they first invented it." David Foot's book was based on tapes Gimblett had left before committing suicide: "Gimmo droning on and on about how awful life is. It nearly drove Footy daft."

Eric had been through a war, and he had come close to death. His perspective had an honesty that I liked.

"There were two things which influenced Harold. There'd been a lot of people saying, 'Bad luck, Harold, you ought to be in the England team.' And that got to him. And he married a woman, Rita, who had pretensions to being a bit posh; she felt that she was a cut above us cricket crowd. So these two things reacted on Harold. And of course he was a prize hypochondriac. I remember one game. I stopped in longer than him and, when I got back to the pavilion, there were five doctors in there. Five of them."

There was no doubt in my mind that Gimblett was a brilliant batsman, a real entertainer. Eric told me of a magnificent innings Gimblett had played at Maidstone: 184 in less than two sessions. "When Gimmo was out, we all used to clear the dressing room. It was standard practice. I was twelfth man, and this chap came up to me. 'I'd like to buy him a drink,' he said. So, when the time seemed right, I went in."

"Harold, there's a bloke wants to buy you a drink."

"I don't want a bloody drink."

Eric shook his head and continued telling me the story. "Gimmo started on about the bloke the other end not scoring."

"That was a bloody fine innings. Go on, what do you want to drink?"

"I don't want anything."

"Look, just say something."

"Oh, all right, I'll have an orange juice."

Eric went out to find the man.

"Look, I'm sorry," he said. "He's a bit tired. He'd like an orange juice."

"Christ," the man replied. "I wish I could bat like that on orange juice."

Eric was a Taunton boy. His father was a shopkeeper, selling cigarettes and sweets, and Eric spent many boyhood hours at the county ground, part of a group who hung around the pavilion for autographs.

"We got it pretty well sussed out: which ones would sign, which ones were better asked after they'd been in, how to avoid the blokes who used to chase us away. I even got W.R. Hammond, and he would never sign anything. I was on the ground early, on my own, and I saw him in the pavilion, still in his civvies, smoking. So I went up to him. I said, 'Excuse me, Mr Hammond' – they always reacted better if you asked them by name – 'may I have your autograph?' And he signed. And his ash dropped into the book. I kept the page very carefully after that.

"One year my father gave me this posh album for Christmas. I was waiting outside the pavilion, and Frank Lee came out and signed it. 'That's a nice book, isn't it?' he said. 'I'll keep it for you and get all the others to sign it.' So he kept it the whole bloomin' season and got all the counties to sign. What a disaster! They didn't count, you see. I hadn't collected them myself. None of them counted."

Maurice Tremlett was Eric's great friend. Tremmy, as he called him; they were only four days apart in age. Maurice's father was a post office clerk, his mother a customer in the shop. Now the two of them were making their debut in the same match at Lord's, two youngsters in an elderly Somerset side, six of whom had begun their first-class cricket back in the 1920s.

Frank Lee was one of them. Middlesex born, he had made his first appearance at Lord's in 1923, the year of Eric's birth, playing for the Young Professionals of MCC against the Young Amateurs. I found an account of it in his book 'Cricket, Lovely Cricket'. In it he described his first-ball duck from the moment he stepped out of the pavilion: 'Absolute fright must have overcome me, for it appeared to me that I was watching my ghost walking to the middle, a feeling which rapidly dispersed when I heard the clatter of my falling wicket, when deep shame replaced it.'

Eric went out to bat at number seven on Monday morning. Middlesex had made 231, and Somerset were in trouble at 68 for five. "Clench your teeth when you first go in," Frank Lee suggested kindly.

"Bill Edrich was bowling. He was a round-arm slinger. About three times as fast as anybody I'd ever faced before. And he was swinging it. I missed the first ball completely, and it swung past the off stump. The second one was straight. As I walked off, I heard Jim Sims saying, 'Well bowled, William.'"

Hill, bowled Edrich, 0. Or should that read Flying Officer E. Hill, D.F.C., D.F.M., bowled Squadron-Leader W.J. Edrich, D.F.C., 0?

Edrich had won his Distinguished Flying Cross as a bomber pilot taking part in low-level raids on German positions. On one occasion, empty of ammunition, he had seen a Messerschmitt close down on him and aim for the kill, only to discover that the German too had no firepower.

Eric had won his medals as the navigator of a Mosquito on 53 missions, none more dramatic than the sortie beyond the Lofoten Islands off Northern Norway in July 1944.

My head was full of cricket when I met Eric that first time, and I did not ask him much about it. By the next year, however, I had come to realise more clearly how important his wartime experiences had been. So I returned to 'Pennypiece', and I asked him to tell me in full detail about the sortie.

The German battleship *Tirpitz* was threatening vital convoys heading for the Russians, and the Norwegian resistance had lost track of it.

North Norway was at the extremity of the Mosquito's range, the fuel tanks only just adequate. Three days earlier, they had set out in search but had found no sign of the *Tirpitz*; the following day, another crew hit bad weather and were killed as they crashed into Scottish mountains. Eric and his pilot, Frank Dodd, did not need to be told that their mission was a perilous one.

They refuelled on Shetland, and after a long flight they located the *Tirpitz*, descending for close-up photographs. Then the German fire began. "Frank did a quick turn, and the perspex bubble top of the cabin blew off, with all the maps, the navigation bags, the telegraph equipment." Open to the wind and not far from the Arctic Circle, they returned for more pictures, then away they went. Cloud everywhere.

They were desperate for navigational help – but their answering code was lost in the sea. "I sent them our names, ranks, service numbers, but they just used the code 'Challenge'."

For over four hours they flew above the clouds. Not wanting to go down and use up precious fuel. Not knowing if they were still on track.

"Frank wasn't much of a talker," Eric said, "and I suppose I wasn't either. We were both trying to disguise our fear. I remember it being very tense."

A brief break in the clouds revealed an unusually still sea, and that was good news for their fuel consumption. "We were both thinking what we would have to do if we ditched, but neither of us said a word about it. The hardest thing was trying to think of something to do to divert our attention."

It was over nine hours since they had left Shetland, and for four hours they had flown with no top on the plane. The fuel gauge was steadily dropping down towards empty. Minute by minute the sky was growing darker.

"We decided to go on until it was absolutely critical or until we could see something. Then I saw this gap in the cloud, and I said, 'Frank, there's land.' We went straight down onto an airfield near Wick."

Over lunch Dorothy said how Eric should have written a book. He had so many good stories, and he had stayed in the game as a reporter. At the time I thought it wasn't a viable proposition; he was too minor a character, too long ago. I regret that now. His stories often seemed quite trivial, but they had a freshness and they shone such a bright light on the world as it used to be.

One belonged to a spell of labouring he did to get stronger, loading and unloading lorries at an army supply depot outside Taunton.

"This chap there played for some local team, and he used to sneer at me. He came in one week, said he'd got some wickets the previous Saturday. I said, 'What do you bowl?' 'Oh, all sorts,' he said. 'Well, what's your best ball?' He said, 'Shooters.' I managed not to laugh. 'How do you bowl them, then?' 'I'm not bloody well telling you,' he said."

Another was a story about a game in 1949 against Leicestershire, who were being captained by a young amateur Stuart Symington, a newcomer to the circuit and an opening bowler.

"Gimblett and I got out to him in the first innings, being careless, and Gimmo was furious. As soon as he got in the second time, he started bashing as though there was no tomorrow. And after two or three overs this poor bloke Symington was stood in the middle of the pitch. Just as Gimmo was coming down to talk to me (which was a surprise), Symington starting talking to himself: 'If this is first-class cricket, I've bloody well had it.' Gimmo looked up and said, 'You want to thank your lucky stars Charlie Barnett's given up the game.'

A third story, one that especially tickled me, was about a wartime RAF match against Brize Norton. "We had an officer as captain, a prize prick. As we walked on the field, he produced a new ball. Very few of us had ever seen one before. It might have been a Surridge. 'Who uses a new ball?' he asked. There followed absolute dead silence. 'Well, I've never done it,' I said eventually. 'But I know how you're supposed to do it.' 'Well, I suppose you'd better have a go with it.' I bowled gentle, in-swinging half-volleys, and in no time we had eight wickets down."

"Well bowled," the captain said. "How many have you got?"

"I've got all eight."

"I'll tell you what. You get the other two, and we'll have a big piss-up in the mess. Get the ball mounted. And just to make sure, I'll go on at the other end and bowl wide."

"He went on next over, and he clean bowled the last two. Eight for 26, I took."

The winter of 1946/47 was a hard one. Heavy snowstorms and sub-zero temperatures lasted for weeks, fuel supplies were low and post-war rationing was at its most severe, even the sweets and tobacco in Eric's father's shop. "But he always found things to buy and sell. I think he was the only one in Somerset selling those cartridge cigarette lighters, he had phony cough sweets that were off ration, and of course a lot of dodgy fags. Then he struck up a friendship with a lady who counted the coupons in the Food Office. She and her boyfriend ended up living above the shop."

By contrast, the summer of 1947 was the warmest since 1911, and the cricket certainly lived up to the weather.

I fell in love with that game at Lord's. It was full of the twists and turns of a good cricket match, and it had all the romance of the unfancied Somerset side travelling up to London and taking on the stars of Middlesex. Somerset had not beaten them since 1924, and by mid-afternoon on that Monday Middlesex, building on a first innings lead of 97, had reached 56 for two. Robertson and Compton were going well, and the game seemed to be drifting steadily beyond the grasp of the visitors.

Then came a spell of bowling from Maurice Tremlett that changed not only the match at Lord's but the whole course of the young man's career in cricket. He bowled Compton with a ball that cut back off the pitch faster than the batsman expected, he struck four more times and Middlesex were all out for 78.

"The story went round that Tremmy hit Leslie Compton on the thigh, and Leslie had to go to the doctor to get blood moving through the vein. We thought this was highly dramatic. Even the old 'uns did. It suggested that Maurice was a tremendously fast bowler. He was quick, but he wasn't that quick."

Since the war England had struggled to find new fast bowlers, and the excitement in the press box was palpable. *The Times* called it 'as good a piece of bowling as one could hope to see this summer.'

"A wonderful bit of bowling," EW Swanton told Jack Meyer at close of play. "He's certain to be England's first choice fast bowler for the West Indies tour this winter."

Jack Meyer cautioned against such excess. "He's going to be a batsman, not a bowler. Please don't overdo the superlatives."

"OK," Swanton replied. "I'll keep it toned down."

'Tremlett's possibilities stand out for all to see,' read the supposedly mild version. 'He may become a truly fine bowler.' The headline writer egged it up further: 'YOUNG BOWLER'S AMAZING SPELL AT LORD'S'.

"Frank Gillard of the BBC interviewed him," Eric said. "A curiously starchy sort of interview. 'Is there anything especially you remember about your first bowl in county cricket?' And Maurice said, 'After my first over I found I was unable to speak.' Of course he'd never talk like that normally. Tremmy didn't talk much, anyway. He was just a natural bowler. He ran in. There was no particular artifice."

I found an article that Jack Meyer had written about the game, and about the excitement that followed Tremlett everywhere throughout that summer.

> 'As soon as Wellard and Andrews had bowled a couple of overs each, the shouting would start. "Put Tremlett on. Put Tremlett on. Tremlett! Tremlett! Tremlett!" In due course (perhaps sooner for I do not like playing in front of shouting mobs), I invited Maurice to have a go. On several occasions he refused point blank … He took a few wickets here and there but suffered agonies in the process.'

It was all downhill for Tremlett's bowling. "In the West Indies Gubby Allen tried to get him swinging the ball," Eric said. "He was very different when he came back. Said he'd got a lot to learn about bowling."

Tremlett made a second tour, to South Africa, but within three years he had become a specialist batsman, his rare attempts at bowling greeted now by noisy barracking.

"He was a hero of mine," Ken Biddulph told me, remembering Maurice as the county's first professional captain. "He'd come and bowl in the nets, and he made us all look slow. But he couldn't do it in the middle. He was very self-conscious. Very shy. There was one game when we had a few injuries, and I'd bowled a lot of overs. He was conscious that I was getting tired, and he wanted me to come back later."

"I want to give you a rest, but I don't know who to put on."

"Why don't you bowl a few overs yourself, skipper?"

"Oh, no."

"Come on, you're quicker than any of us. You could shoot this lot out. You won't even need to bring me back. Go on."

"Oh, all right."

"I felt rather pleased that I'd talked him into bowling. He came on, and he bowled three wides in his first over, a couple in the next, and of course there were rumblings in the crowd. So he took himself off. He just couldn't do it."

"With time," Eric said, "I think Tremmy came to realise that, whereas bowling was bloody hard work, batting – which he could do just as well – was a cushy little number comparatively."

By close of play at Lord's Somerset, needing 176 to win, were 101 for five. Neither Eric nor Maurice had batted.

For the first time I was being told about a match played before I was born, and I was spellbound.

They spent the evening in the bar, listening to Arthur Wellard's stories. He was 45 years old by this time, a seasoned professional who had not only played a lot of cricket but had seen a lot of the world.

"He'd coached me before the war. As a boy I'd found his huge frame forbidding. But, as I got to know him, he came to seem like a rather indulgent uncle. He had a sunburnt face that would sometimes fold into a marvellous gutta-percha grin. And his vast hands would demonstrate all the swerves and swings of the curving ball as he told his stories."

I recalled an image Ken Biddulph had once conjured up, of Arthur Wellard and Alf Gover at the table at Alf's cricket school. They would sit in silence, gesticulating to each other. One would be holding an imaginary ball in his hand in the grip of an away swinger, or an off-break, and the other would play the appropriate shot. It would go on for several minutes as the youngsters sat and watched.

"Arthur drank quite a bit," Eric said. "RJO expected his fast bowlers to drink. And we used to get him telling yarns. He was a wonderful yarn-teller. I don't think he realised just how good he was. He didn't have that many stories, but he had half a dozen good standbys."

One in wartime Italy involved trout-tickling in a stream: "We 'ad these 'and grenades, see, and we set off 'alf a dozen of them." Another was of a heavy drinking session by Joe Hardstaff on Lord Tennyson's tour of India.

But their favourite was the one about the night-time tiger shoot in the jungle, on the same tour of India. "The Maharajah of Baroda. Nice kiddy. 'Ad a place upcountry. About the size of Buckin'am Palace. Well, he had this goat tied up in his 'unting 'ide, ready – see – for the tiger."

"That was the one we loved to hear. He used to get us enthralled. He'd never change a word at all. ''Ere,' he'd say. 'I've told you this before, I'm sure I have.' But we'd always find somebody who hadn't heard it and make him go on. And it was always worthwhile. Something would be different. Nothing about the words – but an attitude or a gesture. An odd new inflection in the voice or a new twist to the eyebrow, to send us into stitches."

Finally the tiger would appear, the guns would blaze, and Alf Gover's petrified face would peer anxiously round the hide.

"Blimey, me Lord, you've shot the bleedin' goat."

I was as enthralled as the young Eric had been.

"It wasn't only stories. Arthur talked a lot of cricket, too. It's where us young blokes learned about the game. I learned a lot listening to Arthur."

Harold Pinter wrote a 15-minute radio piece about Arthur Wellard, who in later years had played for Pinter's team of actors, The Gaieties. It was full of Wellard's stories, as well as some lovely exchanges between them:

> "Listen, son, you've got a good pair of forearms. But just because you give one ball the charge and get away with it, doesn't mean you can go out and give the next ball the charge, does it? Be sensible. What do you think the bowler's doing? He's thinking, son. He's thinking. He's thinking how to get you out. And if he sees you're going to give him the charge every ball, he's got you for breakfast. You're supposed to be an intelligent man. Use your intelligence."
>
> "Sorry, Arthur," I said.

Eric was deeply suspicious of anything that involved Pinter, but he soon rang me. "He's got Arthur to a T."

There was a misty, humid haze about Lord's on the Tuesday morning. Jack Meyer hit a lofted drive for four, then lost his off stump. Bertie Buse was caught behind, and Somerset were 113 for seven, needing 63 runs to win. The 46-year-old keeper Wally Luckes was still out in the middle, and he was joined by Eric, demoted from number seven to number nine. The new ball was taken, with only Maurice Tremlett and Horace 'Tubby' Hazell to come. The game was approaching its climax.

I read the reports in the newspapers. Jim Swanton was there for the *Daily Telegraph*: 'Hill faced a nightmare of a situation,' he wrote, 'with 0 in the first innings and Middlesex round his bat like vultures.'

"I was hopeless. I kept playing and missing, over after over, and Wally at the other end kept making these 'keep your elbow up' motions. Well, my bat was straight enough. It just wasn't in the right place. Eventually I got a run, I don't remember how."

'Luckes is a stubborn batsman,' *The Times* reported. 'He refused to be intimidated by the velocity of Gray and Edrich, and he found a sympathetic partner in E. Hill.'

"I straight drove Bill Edrich, and the ball hit one of the block-holes and bounced up over his hand. We ran three. It was my first hit for more than a single, and I began to feel it wasn't impossible to score runs."

They needed 176 to win, and together they took the score from 113 to 151. The misty haze cleared, and the sun shone once more on cricket.

Then the game took another twist. Luckes was caught at the wicket off Gray for 26, Eric caught at slip off the slow left-armer Jack Young for 17. There were still 25 runs to get, and now only Tubby Hazell and the young Maurice Tremlett were left to score them.

They reached lunch with 16 wanted. "We were all smoking like chimneys," Eric recalled. "And I was twittering like an old fool."

Much was expected of the batting of the young Eric Hill. He looked elegant, and he had a good technique. Before the war he had been coached by Arthur Wellard in those afternoon sessions at the ground laid on for sons of members. "At first I didn't like the idea of Arthur," Eric said. "He used to drink and smoke. Then I realised practically all the others did, all except Wally Luckes."

Eric scored runs at Taunton School, leaving at the age of 16 in 1939. Then he scored runs in local cricket in 1940 and 1941, working the first year in his father's shop, the second for the War Agricultural Committee. "I was telling farmers how to run their farms, with all the weight of my seventeen and a half years." He was in the RAF by the summer of 1942, and he was still serving in 1946. So his first summer back in Taunton came in 1947.

He was not taken onto the county's staff, but he was picked in the team for the first game. "There was a sort of understanding that I would be given five matches, but I don't think anything was actually said. People didn't talk about these things so much in those days."

Eric made an unbeaten 32 in his second match, against Warwickshire at Taunton, and 38 against Essex at Ilford in a match he remembered for a whirlwind 67 from the Essex opener 'Dickie' Dodds: "one of the few batsmen who could get Arthur Wellard to call for his sweater."

The five matches produced only 128 runs in all, and he returned to club cricket. Then in 1948 he joined the staff as a professional, taking the place of Frank Lee, now retired, as Harold Gimblett's opening partner. In the fourth match, at Lord's, he made his first fifty – though the achievement was dwarfed by the runs of Edrich and Compton, who on the first day put on 424 in four hours. Harold Pinter had Arthur Wellard talking about the game in the radio programme:

> "We got rid of Robertson, we got rid of Brown, and then these two buggers came together and they must have made about a thousand. I'd been bowling all bloody day, and the skipper says, 'Go on, Arthur, have one more go.' 'One more go?' I said. 'I haven't got any legs left.' 'One more go,' says the skip. 'Go on, Arthur, just one more go.' Well, I had one more go and then I dropped dead."

Wellard, 39 overs, nought for 158.

"When we came off," Eric said, "people said, 'Cor, that must have been tiring.' But it wasn't tiring at all. We were just thanking people for throwing back the ball."

Ever after, when Robertson and Brown opened the Middlesex innings, Horace Hazell would counsel the new-ball bowlers. 'Don't get those other buggers in too early.'

"I thought Jack Robertson was perfect," Eric said. "He was the sort of batsman I'd have liked to have been. He scored 200 against us at Taunton one year, and we'd stopped for a drink after the game. Some bloke came up. 'Cor, that Robertson, I've never been so bored in my life.' It was the most perfect batting I'd ever seen. I only saw him beaten twice."

Eric's father had promised him one hundred pounds when he scored his first century, but the money never became due. His highest score was 85 at Kettering in 1948, he never hit 1,000 runs in a season, and he left the playing staff at the end of 1951. He had not become the player they hoped he would be, not fulfilled the promise Arthur Wellard had spotted back in those pre-war coaching sessions.

"Dear Arthur," Eric sighed. "I fancy my failure to become a better cricketer was one of his real disappointments."

His last game was in early August at Weston, where the committee would meet to discuss contracts for the following summer. "They came out of a pretty bibulous lunch," he said. "A lot of them didn't know a cricketer from a wombat. We had to keep our eyes open when we went in the bar. Make sure they didn't see *us* overdoing it."

He had scored fewer than 500 runs that summer, at an average below 15, so his dismissal was not a complete surprise. "I was expecting it. There was one nice old boy on the committee. He had a shop in Radstock, selling garden rollers and cricket bats and tents. He said, 'I'll speak up for you, Eric.' It was all very well, but he had no knowledge of cricket. He'd just look at a scoresheet and say, 'He's a good player, he made 100.'"

There were almost no cricketers of any substance on the committee, though the President was the former captain Bunty Longrigg. "Bunty knew how to play, but he didn't have much insight. I don't think he had much idea about human requirements or encouragement."

Eric took a position with the *Somerset County Gazette*, reporting among other things on the cricket, and he watched with despair as the county sank into last place in both 1952 and 1953, winning just two games in each of the years. At the end of the second summer he became a prime mover in a protest group, designed to overthrow the committee.

The 1953 rebellion. Eric rang me in 2003, suggesting that I might like to work with him on a little booklet, to mark the fiftieth anniversary. So I travelled down to 'Pennypiece' a third time, and he got out all his old papers.

"What sort of people were on the committee?" I asked.

As always his answer, while short of precise details of names and occupations, captured perfectly what I needed to know.

"They were sound blokes in their own fields, but they reckoned they knew about cricket when they didn't. They were the sort of men who liked to say they were on so many committees – the Conservatives, the British Legion, that sort of thing: 'giving up my time when I could be at home doing the crossword or listening to the wireless.' They were extremely good at passing votes of thanks at the end of the year."

Captains had come and gone, seven in eight years, all of them amateur, and for 1953 they had turned to the Berkshire farmer Ben Brocklehurst. "He wasn't really a good enough player, but by then there weren't the amateurs available. Later on, we found out that, because he'd had to leave his farm, he was being paid to employ a manager in his absence – and paid, I may add, rather more than the professionals were earning."

They advertised for players in *The Cricketer*, other counties were scouted, but the best of the trialists – Devon's Len Coldwell, later of Worcestershire and England – was deemed 'not to be up to standard'.

Three of them started the campaign: Ron Roberts, Bob Moore and Eric. They requisitioned a special members' meeting, held at the Corfield Hall in Taunton, and 350 people turned up, passing a vote of no confidence in the committee. But the committee called a second meeting, what Eric called "a cheaty thing": "On a Friday evening at 5.30 at Weston, when nobody's got cars. They sent out a postal voting form, with a full defence of their own conduct and nothing from us. It cost us 18 quid to get something printed and sent out. Tremmy got half a crown an hour for sending out the committee's thing, then he came into us and did the same thing for nothing."

Fifty years on Eric was still angry about it, and nobody came out of the tale worse in his eyes than Ben Brocklehurst. "All the time he used to say to us, 'Keep going, that's the stuff. Don't blame the players, blame the committee.' Then at Weston the first bloke to get up and speak in favour of the committee, who should it be? B.G. Brocklehurst. He referred to Ron, Bob and me as Faith, Hope and Charity.'

The rebels lost the battle, but they did not lose the war. The three of them were co-opted onto the committee, and Eric was asked to captain a newly-formed second eleven in the summer of 1955. He had the next generation of Somerset cricketers to mould, Ken Palmer, Brian Langford, Graham Atkinson and Ken Biddulph among them. "The first game was down at

Falmouth," he said. "They won the toss and batted. The grass was fairly long, and we had nobody outside slips and mid-off, mid-on. Kenny Biddulph took eight for 38."

I looked it up, and he was spot on. They were in danger of losing, but Eric went in at number eight and scored a resolute and unbeaten 38.

The county was moving forward. Ron Roberts recruited the Australian Colin McCool, the old roustabout Bill Alley arrived from Sydney via Blackpool and the Guyanese Peter Wight from Burnley. People called them the League of Nations, and in 1958 they finished third in the championship table – under the captaincy of a professional, Maurice Tremlett.

At Lord's the bell for the end of lunch rang, and Horace Hazell and Maurice Tremlett returned to the middle, still wanting 16 runs for victory. Hazell struck a four through the covers, then Tremlett coolly sent a ball from slow left-armer Jack Young high into the air over long-off. It landed among the members, and now there were only six runs needed.

"By this stage," Eric said, "I think I was treating it like an ordinary cricket match, not thinking about the importance of it. 'It's here to be won,' that's all."

The batsmen drew closer and closer to victory till finally Maurice Tremlett was back on strike with scores level. County cricket had not seen a debut like it since Harold Gimblett's century at Frome.

Eric reflected for a moment.

"I think we all felt, 'Thank God we got away with the War and we're able to do this.'"

The clouds had cleared; once more county cricket was bathed in sunshine. It would turn into the summer of Compton and Edrich, a golden summer, and it started here in this match at Lord's. 'Test matches may come and go,' *The Times* declared, 'but a county match with a finish so tense and yet so friendly can in enjoyment never be excelled.'

County cricket at its best.

For Eric they were 'good old days', and he could only feel sadness at the decay of the county game, a decay that he had witnessed over a lifetime of playing and watching: the constant tinkering with formats, the gradual switching to the one-day biff-bang, the removal of all the England players, the come-and-go of their overseas replacements, the decline of the camaraderie of the circuit. For the generation brought up on Compton and Edrich, it was painful to live through.

"At my worst moments," he said heavily, "I wish county cricket would stop. That's when I'm really down."

123

He did not linger for long with that line of thought, preferring to praise the emerging talent of the young Marcus Trescothick, who later that year would graduate from Taunton to the England team.

"Let's not get downhearted," he said with a resolute good sense.

Eric moved from 'Pennypiece' into the nearby town of Williton, dying in the summer of 2010. Singular to the last, he requested that there be no funeral, leaving his body to medical research.

The last time I visited him, he was laid up in bed. I took him a copy of a book I had just published, a collection of the cricket writings of his old Taunton School friend, Alan Gibson. It included a tribute to Eric – 'The Lord of the Taunton press box' – as well as some poignant linking passages by Gibson's son Anthony, charting his father's decline into alcoholism.

"Drink was the ruin of him, wasn't it?" I said.

Eric smiled. "Actually, I thought drink was the saving of him."

One to win.

Jack Young bowled once more. The fielders had moved in to stop the quick single, and Maurice Tremlett heaved the ball over mid-on. They needed just a single, but he did what he did when he was playing for Rowbarton Brewery down in Taunton.

"I was so used to the country stuff," he told John Arlott, "that I made poor Horace run three – just to make sure. As we did in village matches."

Wisden confirms his story.

Lord's, 13 May 1947.

Somerset, needing 176 to win, 178 for nine.

The Middlesex players lined up in front of the pavilion, and they clapped in the batsmen. Jim Swanton in the *Telegraph* called it 'a piece of cricket to live long in the memories of those lucky enough to see it.'

Middlesex versus Somerset at Lord's. The fixture had been played 42 times over the years: Middlesex had won 29, and Somerset had now won four.

"Nobody talked about the past in that way," Eric said. "The only thing I remember is the odd time when Arthur would say, 'Oh blimey, we're going to play at so-and-so, I never get any wickets there' or 'I always do well there.' Gimblett knew the history – but he was unusual. For me at Lord's that day, it was just Played 1, Won 1, that's all."

In the dressing room the Somerset team celebrated in the only way they knew. "Whenever we won, Nutty Hazell used to lead us in a rendition of this song, *The Three Black Crows*."

It was an old folk song, originally about three ravens feeding on the carcass of a horse, but in Hazell's version they were black crows flying into a farmer's barn and eating all his corn:

I'll go away and get my gun
An' shoot those buggers one by one.
The more I sows, the more I grows
The more it's eaten by those bloody crows.

"It was a ridiculous thing, but we all used to bawl it out."

Then came the train journey home, with the cricketers disembarking in ones and twos – Bertie Buse in Bath, Horace Hazell in Bristol, Wally Luckes for Bridgwater, Jack Meyer for Street – till there were only the three of them left.

"It was just Arthur, Maurice and me by the time we got to Taunton, and we all repaired to the Crown and Sceptre. Round the corner from Arthur's house in St Augustine Street. Disgustin' Street, as he called it. It was 254 paces from the public bar to his front door."

The regulars gathered round as the three of them, led inevitably by Arthur, told the story of their great victory.

More than fifty years had passed, and now Eric was telling me. He was not a story teller with the panache of Arthur Wellard, but he brought the past alive for me – without sentiment or romance. I learned a lot listening to Eric.

I have learned a lot listening to all the cricketers in this book: to Bomber with his gift of laughter, Arthur with his late-life contentment, Dickie Dodds and his challenging 'message', Geoff Edrich and his wartime hell and, of course, dear Ken Biddulph who began it all. To think that all I asked him for, all those years ago, was half an hour.

"Half an hour? You can't do anything in half an hour."

I can still hear him saying it.

INDEX

Fairfield Books

17 George's Road, Bath BA1 6EY
telephone 01225-335813
website: www.fairfieldbooks.co.uk

Fairfield Books has been a specialist publisher of cricket books since 1997.

This book, published in late 2010, is its 26th title.

The aim of Fairfield Books is to create well-written, well-presented books that are enjoyable to read and that give food for thought beyond the game of cricket.

Seven of its titles have won major national awards, as follows:

Wisden Book of the Year
Stephen Chalke & Derek Hodgson, *No Coward Soul – The Remarkable Story of Bob Appleyard*
Stephen Chalke, *Tom Cartwright – The Flame Still Burns*

MCC/ Cricket Society Book of the Year
Stephen Chalke, *At the Heart of English Cricket – The Life and Memories of Geoffrey Howard*
John Barclay, *Life Beyond the Airing Cupboard*
Anthony Gibson, *Of Didcot and the Demon – The Cricketing Times of Alan Gibson*

National Sporting Club/ Cricket Writers' Club Cricket Book of the Year
David Foot & Ivan Ponting, *Sixty Summers – Somerset Cricket since the War*
Stephen Chalke, *The Way It Was – Glimpses of English Cricket's Past*

Recent publications include:

Patrick Murphy, *The Centurions – from Grace to Ramprakash*
Mark Wagh, *Pavilion to Crease ... and Back*
Peter Walker, *It's Not Just Cricket*

New publications in 2010 are:
David Foot, *Footsteps from East Coker*
    A personal memoir by the acclaimed West Country journalist and writer.
Stephen Chalke, *Now I'm 62*
    The diary of an ageing cricketer.

If you would like more details of any of these, or would like to be placed on the mailing list for future publications, please get in touch.